Thirteen men
did indeed change the world.
They shattered the face
of the ancient world and changed
the course of history.
For these were the apostles of Jesus Christ.
They were men like us. You could
meet them around the corner in an
elevator or at a social gathering.
They had feet of clay. But they
were endowed with a vibrant faith
in the presence of Jesus.
The fascinating accounts
of their strengths and weaknesses
in the pages following can encourage
all who follow Christ.

13 Men Who Changed the World

Who were they?

What were they like?

What made them different?

What did they have that

changed history's course?

Can it be ours today?

H. S. VIGEVENO

GL
Regal Books
A Division of GL Publications
Ventura, California, U.S.A.

Published by Regal Books
A Division of GL Publications
Ventura, California 93006
Printed in U.S.A.

Illustrations
by
Barbara LeVan

Scripture quotations in this publication are from the King James Version. Other versions quoted are:
Phillips—THE NEW TESTAMENT IN MODERN ENGLISH, Revised Edition, J.B. Phillips, Translator. © J.B. Phillips 1958, 1960, 1972. Used by permission of MacMillan Publishing Co., Inc.
NEB—From *The New English Bible*. © The Delegates of Oxford University Press and The Syndics of the Cambridge University Press 1961, 1970. Reprinted by permission.

Acknowledgment is made to Harper & Row, Publishers for permission to include material from *The Waiting Father* by Helmut Thielicke; *The Man Born to Be King* by Dorothy Sayers and *A Man in Christ* by James S. Stewart. The publishers do not necessarily endorse the entire contents of all publications referred to in this book.

Trade Edition, 1986

Library of Congress Cataloging in Publication Data

Vigeveno, H. S.
  13 men who changed the world.

  1. Apostles—Biography. I. Title. II. Title: Thirteen men who changed the world.
BS2440.V46   1986   225.9′22   [B]   86-3209
ISBN: 0-8307-1150-3

  4 5 6 7 8 9 10/93 92

Rights for publishing this book in other languages are contracted by Gospel Literature International (GLINT) foundation. GLINT also provides technical help for the adaptation, translation, and publishing of Bible study resources and books in scores of languages worldwide. For further information, contact GLINT, Post Office Box 488, Rosemead, California 91770, U.S.A., or the publisher.

Contents

Preface

Two lawyers were discussing their case in an elevator. They had just been through a divorce case. One of them said, "There used to be a time when divorce was a stigma. Now it's a badge of honor." The other replied, "What-you-going-to-do? Change the world? You can't change the world."

Thirteen men did change the world. Thirteen men chosen by Jesus of Nazareth. They left the world far different from what it had been before they came. How did they do it? They had no financial backing, no elaborate organization, no social pull, no prestige, no churches in which to worship, no committees. They were outnumbered, persecuted, forbidden to preach, and finally killed.

How did they do it? One answer comes by looking at their lives, by asking such questions as: Who were these thirteen? What were they like? Why did Jesus choose them? These fascinating questions open up for us a study of the apostles—their characteristics and their part in the greatest enterprise this world has ever seen.

"What-you-going-to-do? Change the world?" The world needs changing, and it needs it in our time. As Jesus called the thirteen, so He calls us to change the world by announcing the Kingdom of God.

H.S. VIGEVENO

1

Andrew, the Friendly Apostle

He Used What He Had

He first findeth his own brother Simon, and saith unto him, We have found the Messiah . . . And he brought him to Jesus (Jn. 1:41,42).

He had been listening to John the Baptist. He was one of those who had gone out to hear the wilderness prophet. He heard John point to Jesus and say: "Behold the Lamb of God . . . " (Jn. 1:29). Intrigued and interested he followed Jesus. Jesus saw him following and asked what he wanted. Andrew and his friend said they wanted to talk with Him. So they spent the afternoon together. It must have been quite a talk, for they even remembered the hour it occurred: "It was about the tenth hour" (Jn. 1:39) . . . a significant hour for Andrew, an hour of decision, an hour of opportunity, an hour that was to change his life. He came away with one conviction: Jesus is the Lamb of God; Jesus is the long looked-for and expected Messiah!

And now Andrew could only think of one thing—his brother, Peter. Small wonder—he had lived in the shadow of his older brother since birth! It was always Peter this, Peter that, Peter all the time. Peter, the center—Peter, the star—Peter, in the spotlight. But Andrew knew that Peter had gifts he had not. Therefore his brother must meet Jesus! Therefore Peter must come to the Messiah! "He first finds his own brother . . . . " (Jn. 1:41).

Andrew was the first disciple to follow Jesus, yet he is never mentioned first in any list of the twelve. Peter is always first, and Andrew is second, even fourth in Mark and the Acts. It was probably always so. In school Peter always had the answers. In sports Peter always was the star. Peter always got the beautiful girls. In the fishing business, everything revolved around Peter. He gave the orders and Andrew was in the background doing his job. When Andrew was introduced, it was always: "What is your name again? Oh, yes, you are the brother of *Peter!*" It's not easy to play second fiddle! To play it all your life, day in and day out week after week, month after month, in everything, all the time, to live in the shadow of an illustrious brother.

And now Andrew discovers Jesus Christ. For once he can be the first! For once he can star. If he had been sure the cards were stacked against him, sure that he would have been first had circumstances been different, sure that the whole world was against him, then he would never have invited his colorful brother to meet Jesus. But Andrew was not sour, not surly, not cynical. He had learned to get beautiful music out of second fiddle.

"He first finds his own brother, Simon, and said unto him: We have found the Messiah . . . And he brought him to Jesus" (Jn. 1:41,42). No doubt. No question mark. He was sure. Had he been doubtful, Peter would not have been convinced. Peter was too strong a person to be moved by indecision. So Andrew was positive to the point. "We have found the Messiah."

Now, Peter listened to his younger brother! He did not turn a deaf ear. With all his boisterous personality, with all his colorful spotlight grabbing, with all his fiery extrovert nature, he listened to his younger brother. You see why Andrew must have played a good second fiddle? His life was such that his older brother respected him: the example of that quiet, reliable, humble Andrew. Peter did not laugh. He did not ridicule. He went along to find out: "And Andrew brought him to Jesus." Perhaps Andrew did not have the personality or the persuasion of Peter, but *he brought his own brother!* We might never have had a Peter if there had not first been an Andrew.

We meet Andrew again in the gospels a few months later. A crowd had listened to Jesus for a long afternoon. The hour was late, and the people had to return home. For some it was a long trip. The women were tired already, and the children were getting cross. There was no food nor money to buy food. They did not have enough in their treasury. So the apostles wondered what to do. Then Andrew stepped forward. (The Bible says again, "Andrew, Simon Peter's brother," [Jn. 6:8], identifying him . . . always in the shadow . . .) Andrew said: "There is a boy here who has five small barley loaves and a couple of fish, but what's the good of that for such a crowd?" Then Jesus said, "Get the people to sit down" (Jn. 6:9,10, *Phillips*). And Andrew brought the boy to Jesus—the boy and his lunch—and Jesus multiplied the loaves and the fishes and fed five thousand!

"There is a boy here." There is one incident in the life

of Jesus when the disciples told children to leave Jesus alone. But that cannot be true of you, Andrew, can it? You are always interested in children. You saw the boy in the crowd, alone. You sought him out. You gave him your big, friendly hand. You talked to him about your fishing experiences on the Lake of Galilee. You told him how to look for fish. You told him how to land fish in the boat. You told him about bait, and cleaning the fish, and he took it all in. You told him, too, about fishing for men. And then he had taken his lunch out of his hip pocket, all mashed and messy, and had offered to share it with you.

Smiling, friendly, warm Andrew, quiet, humble. We have met him twice in the Scriptures now. The first time he brought himself to Jesus, then he brought his brother to Jesus, and now he brings a boy to Jesus.

Once more we meet Andrew in the gospels . . . on Palm Sunday, the last week of the Saviour's life. Jesus entered Jerusalem in triumph. Some men of Greek birth have come to Jerusalem. They have come to the Feast of the Passover. They have heard about Jesus. They want to meet Him. They go to Philip, one of the disciples, but Philip does not know what to do. Jesus has never taken time to see Gentiles. His mission has been almost totally for the Jew. Perhaps Philip should ask John or Peter what to do. But no, they will only say (he can hear them now), "Tell those Greeks to go home. Jesus' mission is for Israel only. He does not have time."

The thought strikes him. Why not ask Andrew? Andrew is sensible—he will know what to do. Andrew is friendly—he will give the right advice. So Andrew talks with them. They say: "We would see Jesus" (Jn. 12:21). Andrew doubtless brings them to Jesus, introduces them, and perhaps brings a moment of happiness to Him. Jesus soul is stirred: "They shall come from the east, and from the west, and from the north and from the south, and shall sit down in the kingdom of God" (Lk. 13:29). "And I, if I be lifted up from the earth, will draw all men unto me" (Jn. 12:32).

So now you have met Andrew. Besides being listed with the other apostles, there is no other mention of his name! He appears only three times in the gospels. And when he appears, he is always doing the same thing: he brings someone to Jesus Christ.

He brought himself first. Then he brought his brother, Peter. Then he brought the boy with his lunch. Then he brought the visitors from Greece. Andrew, the friendly apostle. Andrew, the man who introduces others to Jesus Christ. Without him there can be no success. The Andrews bring the Peters. They are not those who get the notices, the publicity, the footlights, the praise. They are not the stars, but the extras. They are not the quarterbacks, but the linemen. They are always taken for granted. "Now, I remember you, you are Peter's brother." They play second fiddle. They are ordinary men. But without them nothing can be accomplished. One-talent men . . . not five, not ten . . . only one. But that talent is given to Christ, and not kept for oneself.

We remember the Peters, but we forget these Andrews. They write no stirring epistles. They preach no great sermons. They do not win three thousand with one message. They work no miracles. But they bring the Peters who write the epistles, who preach the sermons, who win three thousand, who work the miracles in men. We remember Peter, but we forget Andrew.

Who brought John Knox, the great Reformer? Do you know? I don't. A certain Dominican friar introduced him to

Jesus. I don't know his name, but I remember Knox! What was the name of that substitute preacher on that snowy day in that remote village in England? That day he introduced Charles Spurgeon to Jesus. What was his name? I don't know. We remember the Peters; we forget the Andrews.

But Jesus chose Andrew. He chose him first. Why? Because one-talent men are indispensable to the Kingdom. Nothing can be done without those friendly folk, those humble people, who are always introducing others to Jesus. Once in awhile you get a Peter, a Luther, a Carey, a Spurgeon, a Graham, and mass evangelism has its place; but the most effective way is person-to-person, one by one. In God's plan nothing can be done without Andrew. God needs one-talent Andrews.

Everyone can't be a Peter. But everyone can be an Andrew. This is why Jesus chose Andrew. This is how the 13 changed the world. And that, in fact, is all there is to it. That is how it is done. Nothing complicated about it. Christianity spread over the Roman world as one by one, men were confronted by Jesus Christ—not through great oratory but by personal, dedicated, friendly witness.

In the early days of Methodism there was a like fire! There was a time when the aristocracy would not employ a Methodist cook. The cook would seek to convert the housemaid, the kitchen-maid, the parlor-maid, the between-maid, and everybody else. I doubt if any person hostile to Christianity would hesitate to employ a Methodist today, or a Lutheran, or a Presbyterian, or even a Baptist, on the ground of his religious enthusiasm. A devoted Communist on the campus is given a list of several students he must seek to win to Communism. Few of our Christian students have that desire. But the early Christians turned the world upside down, going from person to person, always introducing men to Jesus, following the example of Andrew.

Men wanted! Andrews wanted! Not those who are seminary-trained, nor highly educated (though such learning is not to be despised). Not those who have all the answers. But friendly men. One-talent men. Men with a heart, a soul, a passion, a purpose. Men who will talk, live, witness, go, be friendly, tell the story: "We have found the Messiah." Christ calls all Christians to go into the world and proclaim the good news that God has visited us; that God has entered the world in Jesus Christ; that He suffered, died, rose from the dead, and is alive forevermore; that the greatest event of history, the greatest evidence of love has taken place: "We have found the Messiah."

Dr. Clarence Macartney, a great preacher of the last generation, illustrates a sermon on Andrew with this vision: "I saw the King seated upon his throne. On either side of the throne, I saw the great angels: Uriel, Raphael, Michael, Gabriel. Before the throne stood another angel: the angel of the Book. And by his side stood one of the mortals. 'Who is this that you have brought, and what are his claims?' asked the King. 'O King, this man was a great inventor, and shed light on the pathway of man through the world.' 'Then,' said the King, 'send him up and let him stand here by Uriel, the angel of light.' So he went up.

"And the angel brought another man before the throne. 'Who is this and what are his claims? This man was a great philosopher, who thought Thy thoughts after Thee . . . . '

"And the King looked at him and said: 'Send him up and let him stand here by the side of Raphael, the angel of Reason.' So he went up and stood by the side of Raphael.

"The angel brought a third mortal before the throne. 'Who is this, and what are his claims?' 'This was a great patriot. With his sword he delivered his people out of the hand of tyrants.' 'Send him up and let him stand by the side of Michael, the angel of the sword.' So he went up and stood by the side of Michael.

"And a fourth mortal came before the throne. 'Who is this and what are his claims?' 'This man sang holy songs in praise of God; songs which still echo through the Church of the living God.' And the King said: 'Send him up and let him stand and sing here by the side of Gabriel, the angel of holy song.'

"Then the angel brought another before the throne. I wondered who he was and why he had been brought. In his person there was no note of greatness. In his eyes no flash of genius. The King said: 'Who is this and what are his claims?' Then the angel looked in the Book, and lifting his head said: 'This man won a soul for Christ.' And I never heard what the King on his throne said, for all heaven rang with a great shout, angels and archangels, cherubim and seraphim, and all the host of the redeemed, rejoicing over the one soul that had been redeemed."

"He that winneth souls is wise" (Prov. 11:30). That is the only way to change the world: friendly Andrews, one-talent men.

Andrew, where are you?
There are people waiting to meet your Jesus.

*   *   *   *   *   *   *   *   *   *   *   *   *

We hear nothing about Andrew in the history of the Early Church. He passed into obscurity. But then, he was never in the limelight anyway. From the first day of Peter's discipleship it was always "Peter, Peter, Peter . . . !" He was always elbowed out by his aggressive older brother.

According to legend he travelled to Greece and preached in the province of Achaia. There he became a martyr and was crucified on an X-shaped cross. Centuries later his relics were taken to Scotland. The ship which bore them was wrecked in a bay, which they subsequently called St. Andrew's Bay. The mariners reached shore and introduced men to the Saviour. Andrew became the patron saint of Scotland.

When the Union Jack was first put together for the British Isles, they placed St. Andrew's Cross on the bottom—a diagonal white cross on a blue background. St. George's Cross of England and St. Patrick's of Ireland were on top, but Andrew's was on the bottom. Friendly Andrew is the basis for evangelism. That's how the apostles "turned the world upside down" (Acts 17:6).

2

Philip, The Practical Apostle

The Practical Man

Philip, he that hath seen me hath seen the Father (Jn. 14:9).

Have you seen him at the supermarket? He is tall, young, good-looking, well-dressed. He pushes a cart in front of him as he carefully eyes the products on the shelf. It all looks a little ridiculous. Instead of pushing that cart, you have the feeling he ought to be out playing basketball, or swinging a tennis racket. In his hand he has a list. He looks it over again and again. He could not go to the store without that list, for after each item is placed in his basket, he takes the pencil out to cross that item off the list.

Should you wish to know a little more about this good-looking grocery shopper, then follow him past the check-out girl to his car. You will notice it's quite clean. He is a careful driver. He never takes chances in traffic. You have to admit, though, he knows his way around town. He always takes the shortest route. He seems to have studied all the streets. It's almost scientific precision with him: what light to miss, what stop-streets to avoid, where to circumvent traffic, how to stay out of the rush-hour tie-ups.

Just before he reaches home, a black cat crosses in front of his car. He does not bat an eye. "So what?" he says to himself. "Who's superstitious? Reading tea leaves, gazing at the stars, signs of the Zodiac? Nonsense! Pure nonsense!" Why he wouldn't be caught dead with a rabbit's foot dangling in his rear window. He wouldn't care if six black cats marched in front of his car—on Friday the 13th.

And now, he's home. You will notice his yard is kept neat. His garage is almost flawless. (You can tell a lot about a man by looking in his garage!) After dinner he looks at his watch: 6:15—time for the news. No interruptions now while he takes in the news of the day. The newscast over he may shut the TV off. Nothing much worth while on anyway. And you will never catch him looking at the late show. No, Sir. Tomorrow is another day. A man has to go to work. "Early to bed, early to rise, makes a man . . . " That's his motto.

Engage him in conversation, if you will. He is quite ready to talk with you. Ask him a few questions. See what you can learn about him. Ask him about religion, go ahead, ask him.

"Religion? You want my views on religion? All right, I'll tell you. Like most everyone else, I was brought up in the Sunday School. I had my early training in the Church. I think it's a good thing, too. Children ought to learn about God. Keeps them out of trouble.

"Believe? Believe in God? Yes, I think I believe in God. There can't very well be a world or a universe without some great Being, without a Creator. My parents were very religious. They always went to church. But I can't live off their faith. I can't believe what they believed, because they believed it. I have to find my own way. I have to find out for myself.

"I'll tell you, I'm a pragmatist. You don't know what a pragmatist is? You mean you've never heard of William James, or read the philosophy of John Dewey? Oh, you've heard of them. I see. Well, pragmatism is a practical way of looking at life: Truth must be tested by practice, belief by action. In other words, a pragmatist cannot believe anything that can't be proven. I believe two times two equals four. That you can know. That you can prove. I believe what I can see, what I can feel, touch, hear, know.

"Faith? Well, faith, you can't put your finger on it. What is faith? Some people have it. Some people don't. What do you do if you don't have it? I'll tell you: If I could see for myself, if I could know for myself, if I could be convinced, I would have faith. I would believe. My approach to religion is the practical approach. Prove it to me. I cannot follow something I don't know, something I have not experienced. But if I ever find God, really find God, I tell you, I will be a devoted disciple."

This has been Philip speaking. That's what he would sound like in the twentieth century. And that's what he sounded like in the first century. Philip—the practical apostle. Philip—growing, groping, gaining ground slowly, cautious, careful, full of common sense, meticulous, precise, intensely practical. How do we know? Well, it's all there in the gospels, as he makes his appearance four times.

We first meet Philip in Galilee: "Philip was a man from Bethsaida, the town that Andrew and Peter came from. Jesus decided to go into Galilee. He found Philip and said unto him, Follow me" (John 1:44,43, *Phillips*). Some of the apostles sought out Jesus. Not Philip. No, he was too practical. He would not be taken in by every stir of religion. He had too much common sense to be swept off his feet by some fly-by-night evangelist. He cannot be sure of all the rumors he has heard. Jesus, the Messiah? That's quite a claim. And he is not going to find out either.

"Jesus finds Philip!" It *has* to be that way. Jesus has to take the initiative. They talk. Philip asks some down-to-earth questions. He gets some down-to-earth answers. His little knowledge of the Old Testament (he did pay attention in Sunday School) helps him to understand. And he is convinced. He is ready to start on a new road. He is willing to follow in the company of Jesus. At least, he is willing to try, willing to begin. He has asked some real questions. He has received some practical answers.

Now for once level-headed Philip is jubilant, jubilant enough to go to a friend—his best friend—and tell him about it: "We have found him, of whom Moses in the law and the prophets did write, Jesus of Nazareth, the son of Joseph" (Jn. 1:45). What a careful observation; what a meticulous, almost scientific statement. We have found Him. Moses in the law wrote about Him. The prophets have spoken of Him. He is Jesus. He is from the city of Nazareth. His father is Joseph.

Andrew had sought out his brother Peter and said: "We have found the Messiah" (John 1:41). That was all, that brief statement. Not so the precise Philip: "We have found him, of whom Moses in the law and the prophets did write, Jesus of Nazareth, the son of Joseph." And when his friend makes some objection: "Can any good thing come from Nazareth?"—practical Philip answers him with these words: "Come and see" (Jn. 1:46).

He would never be taken in by a quack. He would never believe superstitious nonsense. "Prove it to me, and I will be a devoted disciple." He has come and seen for himself. And that is his answer now for any inquirer! The experimental approach—the scientific approach: "Come and see." That is all Jesus asks of the inquirer.

So now Philip follows in the company of Jesus. He is chosen as an apostle. He has begun, but he has much to learn. He moves slowly, cautiously. He is never ready to take one step forward, unless he can be sure of his ground. Jesus notices this. He has chosen Him among the twelve, and He is eager for his development.

One opportunity comes when a large crowd has gathered to hear Jesus. It is late afternoon. The people are tired and hungry, the children restless. And Jesus turns to Philip to ask him a question: "Where are we to buy bread to feed these people?" (Jn. 6:5, *NEB*). Why Philip? Because Philip is tense, practical, scientific, full of common sense by nature. But he is in the company of One whom he has confessed as the One "of whom Moses and the prophets did write." Will he trust that One? Is he ready to rely on Him? What will Philip say?

Jesus asked Philip to prove him, to test him, to see his development. Would he be so cautious and reserved? Would he abandon himself to the Messiah? Would he act on faith—or reason? Tests come in strange ways, at odd moments. Only afterwards we sense that we have chosen, and then—it may be too late.

Philip muffed his opportunity. With his business eye he scanned the crowd. Hmmm . . . ten . . . twenty . . . thirty . . . fifty dollars "would not buy enough for every one of them to have a little" (Jn. 6:7, *NEB*). From the practical point of view, it looked impossible. Where shall we get fifty dollars? There is no way. But he forgot the One whom he saw healing the people of all manner of diseases. He forgot Jesus Christ. He still has so much to learn, this level-headed, practical apostle.

"And there were certain Greeks among them that came up to worship at the feast . . . " (Jn. 12:20). It's Palm Sunday now. Some men from a Greek settlement near Bethsaida, from near where Philip lived, came to Jerusalem. "The same came therefore to Philip, saying: Sir, we would see Jesus (Jn. 12:21). Philip was timid. He must look before be leaps. This was a difficult question: Gentiles to see Jesus? Had He not stated He was sent to the house of Israel? What was the practical thing to do? Cautiously, carefully, "Philip cometh and telleth Andrew" (Jn. 12:22). He cannot make up his mind. Andrew makes up his mind for him! "And again Andrew and Philip tell Jesus" (Jn. 12:22).

However, the most convincing look into Philip's character comes a few days later, at the Last Supper. He has followed in the company of Jesus for three years. He has been an apostle. He has been in the inner group. "Come and see," he has said to Nathanael. And he has come and seen for himself. Only, he has seen, but he does not see. He has heard, but he does not understand. He has accepted, but how much does he really know?

It had been a long, hard, uphill road for him. Even now, does he really believe? Has he actually seen God? Can he be sure? Jesus has spoken so much about God. Jesus has tried to make it all plain. Still it is not plain; it is not clear. Everything is still mystery. Philip with his common-sense mind is very much in a fog. There about the table he interrupts the Master: "Lord, show us the Father and we ask no more" (Jn. 14:8, *NEB*).

Thank you, Philip, for asking that question! It shows me that you are groping. It tells me that despite all your three years in the presence of Jesus, you still ask, you still inquire, you still seek. You may show your ignorance; you also show your thirst for knowledge. Thanks, Philip. I am indebted to your practical mind. For you have brought forth the most astounding, the most arresting, the most staggering words in all literature. You have made Jesus say:

"Have I been all this time with you, and you still do not know me? Philip! Anyone who has seen me, has seen the Father" (Jn. 14:9, NEB). There is grief in your Lord's voice. You can hear it. So long has the Master been with you. So little you have grasped. It is so late an hour. And you have understood so little. You have developed so slowly. You have been so cautious, so reserved, *too practical, Philip, too practical—that's your trouble!* "Philip, have you not seen me at work? Do you not remember how men and women have been healed? Do you not recall how I fed the multitudes? Do you not remember how I asked for faith, always asked for faith? Believe me that I am in the Father, and the Father in me, or else believe me for the very works' sake! Come and see, I said to you. And you said it to your friend. Well, Philip, come and see! He who has seen me, has seen the Father."

There is an epilogue to the story of Philip. Not in the gospels, but in a play by Dorothy Sayers*, where we meet him after the Resurrection. He is still in character: cautious, careful, practical. He cannot believe in the resurrection of Jesus. First reports have reached them as they hide from the police. And Philip with his scientific mind is

* *The Man Born to Be King*, pp. 334, 335, Harper & Row.

the first to deny them: "It was a vision, maybe, or a dream. Our Lord is dead."

John who has been to the tomb, but who has not yet seen Jesus says: "Yes, Philip, I said that too, God forgive me . . . Yet did we not see the widow's son raised up and Lazarus called from the grave? And what did our Lord say to you at the last Passover supper?" Philip cannot forget those words. But this is too much! He cries out: "He died, nevertheless!"

Even when Jesus appears to the twelve, Philip cannot believe it. Is it a phantom, a ghost perhaps? Then Jesus reveals Himself as the risen Lord. Finally he is convinced: "Our Master and our friend— . . . dear Lord Jesus." He cannot now deny! You see, he is practical enough to accept the proof, practical enough to submit to the evidence. And I think that after the Resurrection, after his long groping journey from timidity to triumph, Philip finally arrived! "If I could see for myself, I would believe. If I ever find God, I will be a devoted disciple."

In this scientific age, in this age of reason, in this age of humanism, pragmatism and the practical approach, there are Philip's demanding proof, desiring certainty. They seek knowledge. They seek truth. But of all the philosophies of men, of all the systems of thought, of all the approaches to life: whether scientific, educational, romantic, or pragmatic, Jesus Christ gives the most practical answers! That is what Philip found on his long journey. He found in Jesus Christ *all* he looked for, all he had hoped for. Belief was tested by experience: "He who has seen Me, has seen the Father."

And so, to all who inquire, to all who sincerely search, to all who seek truth, the most practical of the apostles gives the most practical of invitations:

Yes, come and see for yourself.

*   *   *   *   *   *   *   *   *   *   *   *   *

At the beginning of Christianity when the Gospel was first preached, the world was overrun with Eastern magicians and soothsayers. They claimed to be able to communicate with a spirit world. They held the theory that man could advance in knowledge by stages and thus draw closer to God. They set up an elaborate spirit world sufficiently shrouded in mystery.

To the practical Philip this was utter nonsense. He made it his business to expose the fallacy, and proclaimed the simple good news with his usual invitation: "Come and see." Tradition places his preaching endeavors among the provinces of Galatia and Phrygia in Asia Minor. He died at Hierapolis, a city near Colossae and Laodicea. These cities are mentioned in the New Testament (Col. 4:13).

Did he die a natural death or was he martyred? And if a martyr, was he stoned or crucified? We are told by Polycrates, bishop of Ephesus during the second century, that Philip was "one of the twelve who lived as one of the great lights of Asia and is buried at Hierapolis with his two aged daughters." Of the manner of his death we cannot be certain.

3

Nathanael, the Visionary Apostle

The Visionary

Behold, an Israelite indeed, in whom is no guile
(Jn. 1:47).

Nathanael was the absent-minded professor among the twelve . . . the mystic, the aesthetic, the other-worldly man, the saint! The kind of person who goes around with his hair uncombed, his shoelaces untied, and his tie out of place. Talk to him and you may think he's off on another subject. He pays little attention to you. He looks right past you. "He's not quite there all the time," you say.

Such a person was this visionary apostle. He dreamed dreams. He saw visions. He lived with his head in the clouds. He built castles in the air. In short, he constantly acted as if he was in love! And, of course, he was in love— in love with a vision, in love with a Person, in love with a Kingdom. Nathanael—the mystic. Nathanael—the visionary, the saint.

In the gospels of Matthew, Mark and Luke, the name of Nathanael does not appear, but the name "Bartholomew" does. In these gospels "Bartholomew" is linked with Philip. In John's gospel "Nathanael" is linked with Philip. He is Nathanael Bartholomew, or Nathanael the son of Tolmai.

How can a person like Nathanael be an apostle? Can he be of any use to the kingdom? He is so other-worldly, so introvertish. Does not the kingdom depend on extroverts, on good mixers, on people who are enthusiasts? For one thing, he is not dependable! Give him a job to do, and you take the chance that it may not get done. He may not even have listened to you. He probably got the details all mixed up. Then he will take his time. He is never in a hurry, slow as molasses, he just plods along. He says he wants to do it. He knows it should be done. But when?

Nevertheless you cannot help but feel that Nathanael gets something out of life. He seems to enjoy it. The practical man hurries along so. The business man is constantly on the move. The average American is tied to a schedule. But Nathanael has no schedule, and no schedule has him! He will not burn himself out.

We can understand that Jesus would choose Peter. He is dependable, a workhorse, a man with spirit, and talent enough for ten. We can understand that Jesus would choose Philip. He uses his head, he has business sense, he is extremely practical. And even Andrew. He may have only one talent, but he is indispensable to the Kingdom.

But why Nathanael, this dreamer, this visionary? So slight of stature, so thin and undernourished, so emaciated-looking, so refined, so professorish! He cannot work like Peter. He cannot use his head like Philip. He was chosen by Jesus as an apostle. And there he goes in

His company, head in the clouds, dreaming dreams and seeing visions—the saint among the twelve.

I think we shall find out why Jesus chose him when we look at our one Biblical source. When the man comes to Jesus, our Lord at once sees him spiritually. He knows what is in him. "Jesus saw Nathanael coming to Him and saith of him: Behold an Israelite indeed in whom is no guile" (Jn. 1:47).

Quite a compliment! A man without guile, without hypocrisy, without deceit, without craftiness. He thinks no evil. He does not look for wrong motives. He does not psychoanalyze you in every conversation. He takes you at face value. That is true of the visionary apostle. He rose so high in heavenly thought, that he had no time for hypocrisy. He was above it, beyond deceit.

However before this compliment we have another insight into Nathanael's character. Philip, his friend, had just met Jesus. How these two ever hit it off as friends, I don't know. Philip was so down-to-earth, Nathanael so heavenly-minded. Philip was so practical, Nathanael so absent-minded. Philip had so much common sense, Nathanael was always dreaming. Philip was quick on the trigger; Nathanael was so slow.

Anyway, Philip had met Jesus. He came to Nathanael: "We have found him, of whom Moses in the law, and the prophets did write, Jesus of Nazareth, the son of Joseph" (Jn. 1:45).

"Oh, you have?" said Nathanael, "Philip, I would think it of anyone else, but you, my friend? You with all your common sense, with all your practical approach to life, down-to-earth Philip! You? You are convinced that the law and the prophets are fulfilled in a man you call—what did you call him again—Jesus? You say he is from Nazareth?

Wait a minute . . . *Nazareth?* The Messiah could come from Jerusalem, our capital, or Bethlehem, as the prophet foretold; or even from our proud city by the sea of Galilee, Capernaum. But Nazareth? That insignificant, worthless hole in the ground?

"Remember that sickening little merchant whom we met a couple of years ago? You remember him! He took us all to the cleaners with his inferior products. 'Sale,' he said. That's a Nazarene for you! They're all like that, the whole stinking town. Don't act so shocked. It *does* stink. I remember when I had to go there once. They don't keep their animals off the streets.

"And you stand there and tell me that the Messiah— the Messiah, mind you, who could choose any of our proud cities from Dan to Beersheba, has come from Nazareth? Philip—'can any good thing come from Nazareth?'" (Jn. 1:46).

Nathanael, without deception, without guile—Jesus had said so— was a man full of prejudice! A man may have one virtue, but lack others. He may not be a hypocrite, but he may have hatred in his heart. He may not be crafty, but he may be conceited. He may be a good person, like Nathanael, but he may have the poison of prejudice. Nathanael had no guile, but that did not make him perfect. His bigoted remark stands in Holy Scripture.

How can this be? This man with his head in the clouds? This dreamer? This member of the Church? This Christian? Is he not above this sort of thing? How can he, of all people, be prejudiced? This mystic with head-in-clouds thinks himself a cut above the other fellow. He is better than these others. He has done some reading, while they have been pounding nails or catching fish. He has made some spiritual pursuits, while they are not interested in that sort of thing. He has become a Christian and he knows the Bible a little, while they—they are still sinners. That's how he thinks: the intellectual who disdains the uneducated man, the successful man who looks down on the working class, the churchman who considers himself a cut above these people from Nazareth.

But what to do with prejudice? "Philip saith unto him, Come and see" (Jn. 1:46). No argument. Come and find out. Square off against your prejudice. If you want to condemn the whole town because of one man, meet another man from that same town. See if you do not change your mind now. Come to Jesus Christ. He will remove your prejudice. He will show you that the God who has made of one blood all nations of men, has with the blood of One, redeemed all who will come to Him! Come and see Jesus Christ. How He will shame you when He says: "Behold an Israelite indeed, in whom is no guile" (Jn. 1:47).

How could He say that of you, Nathanael? How could He have such a high opinion of you? If only He knew what you had just said about Him. If only He had heard you as you vented your feeling about these Nazarenes. But Nathanael, He does know. He knows more about you than you dare to believe. He knows your heart. He knows what is in you. He knows all. You cannot quite make Him out, this Nazarene. He has surprised you.

You ask a question: "How can you know me" (Jn. 1:48, *Phillips*). You had never seen Him before. You had never met Him. Or had you? Maybe it was in one of those absent-minded moments? What is that He is saying? His voice wakes you out of your dreams.

"Before Philip called you, when you were underneath that fig tree, I saw you" (Jn. 1:48, *Phillips*). He saw you! You did not see Him. You were sitting there, meditating, thinking of God, gazing at the clouds. The eye of Jesus followed you where no natural eye could see. The eye of Jesus penetrated your inner being. He saw your moral self. And therefore He made that astounding statement: "An Israelite indeed, in whom is no guile" (Jn. 1:47). He saw into your heart.

What had Philip just said about Him? The One of whom Moses wrote? Of whom the prophets spoke? The Messiah? And His knowledge of you, there under the fig tree. Something good has come out of Nazareth. You take it all back. You should not have said it. You should not have been so prejudiced. "Master, you are the Son of God! You are the King of Israel" (Jn. 1:49, *Phillips*).

Nathanael is quick to believe, but then a visionary needs little evidence. He is not like Thomas, the skeptic. He is not like Philip, so practical that he must look before he leaps. He leaps before he looks.

Jesus Himself is amazed. The conversation has hardly begun! The man is so quickly convinced. There has been so little evidence. "Do you believe in me," replied Jesus, "because I said I had seen you underneath that fig tree? You are going to see something greater than that! Believe me." He added, "I tell you all that you will see Heaven wide open and God's angels ascending and descending around the Son of Man!" (Jn. 1:50, 51, *Phillips*). Nathanael, you dreamer, you will dream dreams. Nathanael, you visionary, you will see visions. You will see heaven open. You, with your head in the clouds, you will see angels. You, in all your meditation and prayer, you will never reach higher than when you behold the Son of Man in all His glory and truth.

No . . . perhaps Nathanael will not be a great worker in the Kingdom, nor a great preacher, nor a Peter, a James, or a John. He lives too much in heaven already. But he can be an apostle. And as he follows in that select company he reminds us that the first duty of man is to respond to God, to save one's soul, to see visions and dream dreams, to live a life without guile and deception, to advance toward the purity of Christ, to be a saint!

Nathanael is the forerunner of all those sensitive spirits who seek communion with the Eternal Spirit. He is the Francis of Assisi, the Thomas á Kempis, the Meister Eckhart, the William Law. He is the Quaker Thomas Kelly, who says: "It is an overwhelming experience to fall into the hands of the living God, to be invaded to the depths of one's being by His presence." He is the forerunner of God-possessed men.

Nathanael answers the question the world most wants to know: Are there any saints? Can a man be changed? Can he be different? Is it possible to live in this fleshy existence, in this corrupted earth in this perverted world, with a sense of God? Are there still some guileless souls, who have child-like faith, who believe enough in Christ to walk with Him? Are there any *true* Christians? We should expect to find them among the apostles, like Nathanael, that God-possessed saint. We should expect to find them today. So may we live. So may we pray, that when we appear before Jesus the Judge of all men, we may hear Him say to us: "Behold, a Christian indeed, in whom is no guile."

* * * * * * * * * * * * *

We have only that one story about this visionary apostle in the gospels, and nothing is said of him in the Acts of the Apostles. What else he said or did, we don't know. Tradition says that he continued as a disciple, but early Church sources are very obscure as to the scene of his labors and the extent of his preaching.

He presumably met death by flogging. His body, being tied up in a sack, was thrown into the sea. According to the words of Jesus, no matter how he died, Nathanael would see "greater things." He already has.

4

Matthew, the Rescued Apostle

From Means to Meaning

*I am not come to call the righteous, but sinners to
repentance (Mt. 9:13).*

He sat in his booth by the side of the road. His toll-
booth, located on one of the main roads from Damascus
into Israel, was on the outskirts of Capernaum. It was a
good station. Besides regular taxes paid by the residents,
travellers had to stop, present their imported products to
the tax official, and pay their taxes before they could go
on.

Now it was almost closing time. He gathered his
papers together, checked the bills, the receipts, and added
the money he had collected. "Hmmm," he thought to himself, "not bad; business is good and getting better every
day. A few more years, and then . . . " He had put his mind
to it early. He had seen it time and time again: money
talks. The man who has it commands respect: money

talks. So he had decided to make money—that was the important thing. He would not become rich, necessarily, but make enough, enough to live well, enough to retire early and enjoy life. And if others could retire at sixty-five, he could make it at sixty.

He was clever enough to do it. He had a mind for figures, mathematics, statistics. They had always thought him clever in school. He was not a man for sports, too slight of stature, not strong enough. He would never make a salesman, he was not the type. They had often remarked about his high forehead, "a sign of wisdom and knowledge," they had said. He knew he was clever, clever enough to make money.

So he had chosen to be a tax-gatherer. Why not? It was a lucrative field. He had heard that tax-gatherers were hard-hearted men, money-hungry men, demoralized men. But it could not be that bad . . . . After all, they were Jews—most all of them were Jews. Just because they worked for the Roman government, just because they collected taxes, this should not make them outcasts. Of course, the people charged these publicans, these tax-gatherers, with taking too much. But who knew exactly how much went for the government, and how much went to them? Some took seven to ten per cent. He would only take the accepted five per cent. That had been established, and after all, a man has to make a living, even if he has to do it by working for Rome!

Furthermore, he was a true son of Abraham. He was proud of his Jewish ancestry. He would always be true to his heritage. He could never deny that, even if he did have to work for the Romans for awhile. It hurt him when he had tried to attend the synagogue. After he had become a publican, they tolerated his presence a few times, but they had been so cold to him. They did not want him in their congregation. He knew it, he felt it, and he had never gone back. Then, he was too busy anyway, too busy with his work. After his retirement he would go back. Then he would say his prayers and do his duty toward God.

Yet, as he sat there, adding up his columns, checking his receipts, almost ready to close up shop, he was discontent. He felt uneasy. It seemed as if from the figures before him, he heard the voices of people. "Robber!" "Thief!" "Crook!" What had that woman said to him today? "Swindler!" "I'm only doing my job," he had replied. "Lady, I'm not getting anything out of this. Somebody has to collect taxes . . . "

So it had been lately, every day. He tried to put it out of his mind, but he could not. Yet he was an honest business man. He was a God-fearing man. This was getting on his nerves. Nobody seemed to understand. And the words rang down the corridor of his mind, like the oft-repeated shrill bell at school: "Robber, thief, swindler, crook."

The public ostracized him. His neighbors shunned him. The church people had made it clear how they felt. They looked down on him as they would a prostitute. That was utterly unfair. "Collaborator with Rome," they charged, "traitor to Israel." But he was not a traitor, and he never would be. Still he had no friend, that is, none outside the circle of other publicans. And yet they were not really friends. He could feel that. As long as he had money, he was acceptable. If he would ever lose it, he doubted if any of them, any one of them would be his friend. They were selfish. They were all out for what they could get. He had had so much more education. He had studied Greek and literature, yet he could never discuss it. All they could talk about was money, and women, of course, but mostly money. Money was basic to everything else.

His head was swimming now. He wondered if he could ever get through adding up the columns, as this afternoon his whole life paraded before him.

And then he saw Him coming. Down the road He walked, a few of His friends with Him. He had seen Him from time to time, the Carpenter from Nazareth. He came to pay His taxes regularly. He was always prompt. Whenever he had told the Carpenter that taxes had gone up for the next year, the Man had looked at him, merely looked—and yet those eyes had spoken volumes—"was it the tax or was it his percentage." But without a word He had turned quietly and gone His way. The next year He would be back with the required amount.

And now He was coming down the road toward his toll-booth. He had heard that Jesus had left the carpenter shop, had gone down to the river of Jordan to be baptized of John. He had come to live in Capernaum. Everybody was talking about it. He had cleansed lepers and healed demon-possessed people. People were coming from all over to see Him and hear Him. He himself had joined the crowd one day. He had wanted to see for himself. He could not quite know what was happening up front when they had brought the paralytic to Him, but he could hear: "The Son of man has full authority on earth to forgive sins . . . " (Mt. 9:6, *Phillips*).

Son of man? Authority to forgive? To forgive sins? He thought of those words now. He was a sinner, he knew that. His whole money-hungry life —his whole "money talks" philosophy—it was not right. He bent over his work again as if deeply engrossed, but he was not thinking of his work. "The Son of man has full authority on earth to forgive sins . . . . "

Then he could feel it. He did not have to glance up. He knew the Teacher, the Son of man as He called Himself, was standing directly before him. Now he had to lift his head. And those eyes that had looked on him many a time before, looked straight at him now . . . straight at him, and through him, and through his books, and through his accounts, and through his empty life.

All of a sudden he felt dirty inside, just plain dirty. He started shuffling his feet, and his hand twitched nervously. Was the Son of man going to call him names, like the rest of them? Then, let Him get it over with! No, instead He smiled, and He said: "Follow me" (Mt. 9:9). Follow Him? He wants *me* to fellow Him? Me, publican, outcast, crook, a thief? He trusts me and wants me to become a disciple?

Matthew couldn't believe his ears. He was overwhelmed at the compliment, overjoyed at being wanted by the Son of man, and suddenly he did not feel dirty any longer. Just clean, forgiven, at peace. "The Son of man has full authority on earth to forgive sins . . . " That was it! He closed his books. He tumbled out from behind his desk. He shut his booth. And so it was that a publican, a gatherer of taxes, an outcast of society, abruptly made up his mind and made a decision that would alter the entire course of his life: from Matthew the publican, to apostle of Jesus Christ!

For Jesus to choose a publican was as "unwise" a choice as any He could make! The public classified taxgatherers with prostitutes. They were dishonest, greedy, money-minded men. They were not fit for the synagogue, nor could they testify in court. Jesus was not blind to these facts. He knew the friends he had, the company he kept, the influence this would have made on his life. He knew the man's ambitions, goals, and desires. Yet when a scribe with social position and professional attainments came to Jesus, our Lord discouraged him from discipleship: "Foxes have their holes and birds their roosts, but the Son of man has nowhere to lay his head" (See Mt. 8:20). But to Matthew no such negativism, only the positive: "Follow me." The qualifications of the past make no difference to Jesus.

He only sees the possibilities of the future. Matthew is sharp, keen, clever, orderly. Matthew has set his goals in life. Matthew will attain those goals. Matthew is disturbed by his life as a publican. Matthew is empty inside. Matthew is already sick of a life that seeks only money. Matthew wants out of his rut! Humanly speaking—a poor choice! Divinely speaking—a magnificent choice! And the proof of that? The Gospel according to Matthew!

The first Book of the New Testament is a product of Matthew and his ready pen. For now whenever Jesus would teach, whenever He would preach, there was Matthew at His side. The pen which once added figures now took it all down. The keen perceptive mind which kept his ledgers now preserves for posterity the Word of God!

And now I must tell you one more thing about this little, clever fellow, who once believed only in the philosophy "money talks." He writes a gospel about Jesus, and he does not mention himself! Peter gets into the foreground, and James, and John, but not Matthew. Humility is a true mark of conversion. There is only one incident in which Matthew is specifically involved. But he is too humbled to put his own name into it! We have to put the pieces together from the gospel of Luke.

Immediately after his conversion, he invited Jesus to his home. It was quite a'feast. Matthew himself is too modest to play it up, but Luke does. All his former friends and acquaintances were there. It was a going-away party.

Matthew at the head of the table, Jesus in the place of honor, and around the table sat all the social and religious outcasts: worldly men, greedy men, money-hungry men, men with stunted minds, sick, hollow and empty men! Matthew had given suppers before, but never with a Man present who could lose His good name. And yet there was nothing in His manner to make any of his guests feel uneasy. If they wanted the friendship of Jesus, if they looked for help, they could find it in Matthew's new-found Saviour!

But the religious leaders heard about it. They came to see what was going on. As the publicans were ever on the outlook for more money, as empty sinners are ever on the outlook for more excitement, so the religious leaders were ever on the outlook for scandal. "Why does your master have his meals with tax collectors and sinners?" (Mt. 9:11, *Phillips*) they criticized. Jesus, who has not condemned one of these outcasts, now turns to the religious people with a forthright answer.

"It is not the fit and flourishing who need the doctor, but those who are ill! Suppose you go away and learn what this means: 'I desire mercy and not sacrifice.' In any case, I did not come to invite the 'righteous' but the 'sinners'" (Mt. 9: 12,13, *Phillips*). That fits me, says Matthew, as he listens with new-found joy. It fits him all right, and that is why he records it following his call. "The Son of man has full authority on earth to forgive sins. I have come to call 'sinners' to repentance."

Matthew has been rescued. Rescued from his sins, yes. Rescued from his empty life, yes. Rescued from his money-hungry life, from his disillusioning philosophy of "money talks." Rescued from a life he had deliberately chosen, and had found unfulfilling, unsatisfactory—

wanting! And Matthew could never get over it. He had found the pearl of great price. Into his narrow life has come the experience of grace and love.

Do you need to be rescued? Rescued from a life of sin? Rescued from a life of selfishness? Rescued from a hard, stubborn philosophy? Rescued from a meaningless, purposeless, empty existence; from a life without God? Do you want "out"? If Jesus could call a clever little fellow like Matthew, then there is hope for you and me. If Jesus could call a despised outcast, a disturbed sinner like Matthew, then He opens the door to all; then He has indeed come to "call sinners to repentance."

Matthew would say it to you with all his heart. "The Son of man has full authority on earth to forgive sins." He knows whereof he speaks. He has experienced it—he has been rescued. He knows you can experience it, too. And so he must record it in red ink when he takes up his pen to write the gospel: "If a man has a hundred sheep and one wanders away from the rest, won't he leave the ninety-nine on the mountainside and set out to look for the one who has wandered away? Yes, and if he should chance to find it I assure you he is more delighted over that one than he is over the ninety-nine who never wandered away. You can understand then that it is never the Will of your Father in Heaven that a single one of these little ones should be lost" (Mt. 18:12-14, *Phillips*).

> *No, not even Matthew,*
> *And not even you!*

*   *   *   *   *   *   *   *   *   *   *   *   *

Early Church leaders tell us that after the resurrection of Jesus, Matthew preached to the Jews. This we can believe. Even if history tells us little, the Gospel according to Matthew gives all the clues.

Matthew presents Jesus as the Messiah, the promised Deliverer of Israel. He is the son of Abraham, the son of David, the Son of Man who fulfills the prophecies of the Old Testament. How carefully this fulfillment of prophecy is spelled out by Matthew. He abounds in quotations from Moses and the Prophets. Jesus is the King of the Jews. The kings of the East come to worship Him, and Pilate acknowledges His kingship with the placard: THIS IS JESUS THE KING OF THE JEWS.

To Matthew Jesus is the Jewish Messiah. He writes his gospel in Hebrew. And, according to tradition, he takes his own people as his mission-field and dies a martyr's death in Ethiopia.

5

Simon, the Zealous Apostle

The Zealot

And a man's foes shall be they of his own household
(Mt. 10:36).

"It is the fashion of biographers in our day, writing for a morbidly or idly curious public, to enter into the minutest particulars . . . of personal peculiarity . . . The writers of the gospels were not afflicted with the biographic mania"* In fact, we are hard put to it. As far as some of the twelve apostles go, there is little or nothing said about them. One of those is Simon, number eleven on the list. Number eleven, and you see, rather obscure.

There are in the listing of the twelve apostles two men named Simon. The first is Simon, called Peter. Everybody knows him. Peter, the big fisherman; the spokesman for the twelve, the foremost of the apostles. The other is

* *The Training of the Twelve*, A. B. Bruce, T. & T. Cark, 1906.

number eleven, followed only by the name of Judas Iscariot. He is called Simon, the Canaanite. This distinguishes him from Simon, called Peter. As Simon Peter is famous, this Simon, the Canaanite, is obscure. Let us see if we can lift him out of obscurity and find out what he is doing among the twelve, these twelve who changed the world!

He is called Simon, the Canaanite. This may mean that he is from Canaan, the land of Israel, but that does not say anything. Most scholars think that "Canaanite" means something else. They find the clue in Luke's gospel, where he calls him, "Simon, called Zelotes" (Lk. 6:15). Zelotes was a nickname. It identified Simon with a party called "the Zealots." This was a political party. The Zealots were fanatic patriots. They were a group of Jews who believed in national freedom for Israel—no compromise with Rome. This party came into existence about twenty years before the ministry of Jesus. It continued in force after His death. It became so strong that historians say the Zealots were the cause of the overthrow of Jerusalem in 70 A.D. They brought Rome against Jerusalem some forty years after the death and resurrection of Jesus.

Simon Zelotes—or Simon, the Zealot—was a member of this party. He was a member before becoming an apostle of Jesus Christ. That's why they nicknamed him Simon, the Zealot. He was originally one of that band of freedom-fighters, rebels, patriots, who were zealous for Israel. Such zealous patriots have been recently heard from in our world. Freedom fighters in Hungary, Poland, Greece, Burma, Nicaragua and El Salvador, and all through the fermenting continents of the world. These were men of Israel, zealous for Israel, who wanted national, political and religious independence for their country!

Now, I have to admit to you that this is all we know

about Simon. This is all the gospel tells us about him. Yet, on that one word we can build a character. On that one word we will build a personality.

Simon chose to listen to Jesus of Nazareth. Why? How he came to know Jesus we do not know. But why did he choose to follow Him? Was it because the Zealots had no leader? Was it because he felt that Jesus would be an adequate leader? Did he know that Jesus went into the temple and cast out the money-changers? Did he hear the fiery, challenging, gripping preaching of this prophet from Nazareth? Did he think that Jesus was the Messiah? Were the rumors strong in Galilee? Perhaps the Messiah had arrived. Then the Messiah would reign! The Messiah would establish the throne of Israel! The Messiah would bring freedom from Rome! The Messiah . . . a true leader for the Zealots.

Simon was not alone in that thought. The people hoped for the Messiah, also. The people wanted to hail Jesus as King. They cheered the conquering hero as He entered Jerusalem on Palm Sunday. They expected a visible overthrow, a revolution. The apostles themselves looked for it. Even *after* the Resurrection they asked Jesus: "Will you at this time restore again the Kingdom of Israel?" (See Acts 1:6).

So, Simon may have chosen Jesus with the expectation of political victory with the hope for freedom. But if it is not so strange that Simon should choose Jesus, how strange that Jesus should choose Simon! Jesus deliberately chose the twelve from among many followers. Why this Simon from the Zealot party? Why this fanatic patriot? Why this hot-blooded rebel? How different were the aims of Jesus and Simon. Simon wanted political victory. Jesus would soon enough teach: "Render unto Caesar the things

which are Caesar's" (Mt. 22:21) with no thought of overthrow. Simon wanted the kingdom to be restored to Israel,
but fast! Jesus would soon enough say to him: "The Kingdom of heaven is like yeast, which a woman took, and
mixed with three cups of flour and the dough was put into
the oven, until the loaf was risen and baked . . . " (See Mt.
13:33, *Phillips*). It would take time, plenty of time. Simon
relied on the sword, the dagger, the weapons of war. Jesus
would soon say to them all: "They that take up the sword
shall perish with the sword" (Mt. 26:52). So different
were the aims of these two. Why choose him at all?

Besides, Jesus ran a risk with this member of the
Zealot party! Even if he had left the party, it was a risk.
Probably he had left it but, Jesus would always be under
suspicion. "Do you not have among your followers one ot
those freedom-fighters, one of those who wanted to overthrow Rome, one of those Zealots?" It was risky business
to choose this Simon. Of course, it's also risky business
for Jesus to choose us!

Jesus chose Simon, the Zealot, for yet another reason:
He wanted variety, diversity in the group. Not all of them
were to be middle-class, average income, grey-flannel-
suit, respectable citizens of society. He chose the twelve
from many different groups.

Compare Simon and Matthew. Simon, the Zealot, who
wanted to overthrow the Roman government and Matthew, the tax-gatherer, who worked hand-in-glove with
Rome. Simon, the tax-hater and Matthew, the tax-
collector. Simon, the Jewish patriot, and Matthew who
seemed to everyone unpatriotic. Can you imagine these
two hotheads in the same group? But so it is in the
Church, variety, opposites together in one body.

Still there is another reason why Jesus chose Simon,

and this reason towers above them all. Jesus chose the Zealot because, as his nickname implies, he was a man of zeal. He was a man of fervor, sometimes fanatical devotion, eager, hot-blooded, a man with a consuming passion, a man in pursuit of a goal. Jesus wanted him in the Kingdom. Jesus wanted such zeal in His group. If that unbounded enthusiasm could be harnessed, if that passionate zeal could be put on the right track, what a firebrand, what a "freedom fighter" this man would make! Therefore He chose this good soldier with a deep sense of loyalty to a cause . . .

Someone has given this counsel to young people: "Lay up in your youth a large stock of enthusiasm, for you will lose a good many of them on the way." Does that sound cynical, or is it born out in practice? Youth? Youth will tackle the impossible, move the immovable, change the unchangeable. And adults? Adults have a tendency to put enthusiasm into cold storage, into deep freeze. They said of one church in the New Testament: "You have lost your early love" (Rev. 2:5, *NEB*). That church went, bankrupt on zeal.

And so Simon followed Jesus. As he followed he began to change. His political ambitions mellowed in to peaceful ambitions. His military mind became a missionary mind. His aims and motives became the Master's. At first he had heard Jesus say: "Think not that I am come to send peace on earth: I came not to send peace, but a sword" (Mt. 10:34). If any saying of Jesus must have struck Simon liked thunderbolt, it must have been this one. Here is the program of the Messiah. Here is the Zealot's motto—"not peace but a sword." But as he listened to Jesus, he came to understand these words.

The gospel cannot come peaceably. The world is in

darkness and Christ is the light. Darkness and light are in conflict—that is a sword. The world is "antichrist" and Christ is sworn to destroy antichrist. That is conflict—and that is a sword. The sword of Christ is His teaching, His word for our world, and it brings division: "I am come to set a man at variance against his father, and the daughter against her mother, and the daughter in law against her mother in law. And a man's foes shall be they of his own household" (Mt. 10:35,36).

Simon must have experienced this, too. Particularly if his family was pro-Zealot, if his father and his brothers were also freedom-fighters. If they now still belonged to the Zealot party and he had left the party, his own household would have turned against him. His former friends still relied on the physical sword, while he, Simon, relied on the sword of truth. He had been converted.

And now—this is the point—as Simon was zealous for his party, so he became zealous for the Kingdom of God. Simon saw in Jesus a man who held no political campaigns, who began no economic reforms, who instigated no national revolutions. And his zeal grew: his zeal for the peaceful Christ, his zeal for the compassionate Christ who gave His life for the sheep, and who by love sought to enter the hearts of men.

Jesus lifted the sight of Simon, the Zealot. He lifted it from seeing the kingdom of Judea only, to see the Kingdom for the whole world. He lifted it from a narrow patriotism to a broad passion for all men. He lifted it to a Cross by which He would move the world. And that Cross moved Simon to a tremendous zeal, so that he, too, gave his life as a martyr for the Kingdom. Tradition says he died by crucifixion.

Simon, the Zealot. Only one word describes him, but

this nickname follows him even today. A man of daring, vision, enthusiasm; the hot-blooded firebrand among the apostles—a risk. Jesus uses men like that, and He is willing to take that risk on us, now! "He that takes not his cross and follows after me, is not worthy of me" (Mt. 10:38). I think Simon liked that. He was moved by that, and to that Christ he could give his life gladly, zealously. Can you? Does He move you to action?

6

James, the Unknown Apostle

The Unknown Christian

Rejoice because your names are written in heaven
(Lk. 10:20).

When your name gets into the Bible and they tell the
world that you are the son of a certain man, and you are an
apostle of Jesus, but that is all they tell, then that is not
very much information. That is the unfortunate situation
of James, the less, or James, the little, or better, James II.
His father was named Alphaeus. His mother was a follower of Jesus. He, James, was one of the apostles. And
that is all we know. He is listed among the twelve. His
name does not appear anywhere else in Scripture.

The other James among the twelve, James, the
brother of John—of him we learn quite a bit, but nothing
about James II. Not even one word like the word "Zealot"
which described Simon. Not even one question which he
asked Jesus; nothing at all. James II is of all the apostles

the most obscure. He remains in the shadows. He never achieves biblical fame. He is the unknown apostle. Nevertheless . . . he was an apostle, and thereby hangs a tale.

James, too, is a patron saint. I mean "patron saint" in the Protestant sense: a representative, not someone to pray to. He is the saint of the unknown, of the numberless ones, of the nameless millions who follow Jesus Christ.

"As for those who had been scattered, they went through the country preaching the Word" (Acts 8:4, *NEB*). Those who? Who were they? What were their names? Who were these hundreds, these thousands, who spread the Christian faith, who brought the good news of Jesus Christ to men, whose names are not recorded? Paul, we know, and Peter, we know, but who are these? What were the names of those thrown to the lions, those valiant Christians who loved not their lives to the death? Name one. In the long history of the Church, Augustine, we know; and Luther, we know; Calvin, we know; and Wesley, and . . . and . . . how few we really know!

For every general there are probably ten thousand privates. James, apostle unknown, is a symbol of the privates in God's army. But he is an apostle, and thereby hangs a tale, indeed. Why were the rich, the influential, the famous, the successful not chosen by Jesus? Why were Nicodemus and the rich young ruler not in the company of the twelve? Why a fellow whose name is James (James who)? Why are many called, but few chosen?

"Though the burden of the whole world lay heavy upon his shoulders, though Corinth and Ephesus and Athens, whole continents, with all their desperate need, were dreadfully near to His heart, though suffering and sinning were going on in chamber, street corner, castle, and slums, seen only by the Son of God—though this immeasurable misery and wretchedness cried aloud for a physician, He has time to stop and talk to the individual. He associates with publicans, lonely widows, and despised prostitutes. He moves among the outcasts of society, wrestling for the souls of individuals. He appears not to be bothered at all by the fact that these are not strategically important people, that they have no prominence, that they are not key figures, but only the unfortunates, lost children of the Father in heaven. He seems to ignore with a sovereign indifference the great so-called 'world historical perspectives' of His mission when it comes to one insignificant, blind, and smelly beggar, this Mr. Nobody, who is nevertheless so dear to the heart of God and must be saved!"* And that is why He chooses us. That is why you and I—nobodies—can be in His company, too!

James, chosen by Jesus, walked in the company of Jesus. That sends the mind reeling, and the imagination roaming. "Blessed are the eyes which see the things that ye see:" he heard Jesus say, "For I tell you, that many prophets and kings have desired to see those things which ye see, and have not seen them" (Lk. 10:23,24).

He saw Him heal the sick, cast out demons, raise the dead. He saw Him walk on the water. He saw Him feed the multitudes. He saw Him cleanse the temple. He heard Him teach. He heard the sermon on the mount. He heard the parables. He heard the stabbing remarks of Jesus, the kind words, the encouraging words. He was there at the Last Supper. He was there in the Garden. He was there in the City during the Crucifixion. He was there at the Resurrection. He was there for the Ascension.

---

*Helmut Thielicke, *The Waiting Father,* pp. 88, 89.

You envy him? You are not in the company of Jesus? Why not? He is "the same yesterday, and today, and for ever" (Heb. 13:8). You do not see Him at work? Why not? Open your eyes to the Kingdom slowly at work in our world, leavening the lump. You do not hear Him preach? Why not? You have the Word of God. You can read and listen and worship. You were not there at the Cross? Why not? "Were you there when they crucified my Lord? Sometimes it causes me to tremble . . . . " You can have that experience. This unknown apostle, James, has nothing on you!

He was chosen to see, to hear, to walk, to witness. "The Lord . . . sent them off in twos as advance parties into every town and district where he intended to go. 'There is a great harvest,' he told them, but only a few are working in it—which means you must pray to the Lord of the harvest that he will send out more reapers. Now go on your way. I am sending you out like lambs among wolves" (Lk. 10:1-3, *Phillips*). The twelve were sent out, the seventy were sent out, and side by side with the famous Peter, James, and John, James the less proclaimed the Kingdom. He brought the good news as a witness to cities, towns and villages.

Today's Church seems too much of an institution, where people believe correct things, do correct things, say correct things, but give of nothing that excites the imagination and the curiosity of the man in the world.

Queen Victoria was once asked how long it would take her to get a command to every man, woman, and child in the world. Said she: "Eighteen months." How long has it taken Jesus Christ? But that surely is not His fault!

Presbyterian missionary Samuel Moffett recently compared the Presbyterian record in America with Korea. In

1974 there were one and one half million Presbyterians in Korea. Ten years later, in 1984, there were between four and five million! While Korea was tripling membership, American Presbyterians were losing about one third of their membership and cutting back on overseas missionaries!

A person does not have to be a great pianist, or even a musician, to interest other people in Debussy or Chopin. He only needs an enthusiasm about their music. Anyone can do this! Even this unknown apostle was a witness. That much we do know about him, for Jesus sent the twelve. And he continued a witness until his life's end. Tradition says that he died a martyr, and a martyr is a witness, too.

This unknown apostle, chosen, a witness, also had his name written in heaven. Unknown, but known to God. Unknown on earth, but known in heaven. The disciples returned from their witness-tour rejoicing. "Even the devils are subject unto us through thy name!" And Jesus said: "I beheld Satan as lightning fall from heaven. Notwithstanding in this rejoice not, that the spirits are subject unto you; but rather rejoice, because your names are written in heaven" (Lk. 10:17,18,20). That is true cause for joy! The world does not take note, but God takes note. Nameless ones to men are not nameless to God. He is the God of the individual.

We are familiar with the masters of words: Shakespeare, Milton, Keats, Longfellow. But who are the nameless thousands who reduced guttural sounds into a written language? Who invented and perfected the alphabet, laid down the rules of grammar and gave us languages? Their names are unknown to us, but without them the masters of literature could never have written a line.

We know the giants of music: Bach, Beethoven, Mozart, Verdi. But who captured the sounds of nature? Who translated them into notes, composed the scale, and gave the tools to the musicians of the world? Nameless thousands.

Ever so often another of Hollywood's luminaries puts his or her hands, feet, and what have you, in the cement of Grauman's Chinese theater. They are thrilled, they tell the public, because their handprint, footprint and imprints are now immortalized forever, permanently, in the concrete of Hollywood Boulevard. Immortalized? Forever? Permanent? Concrete? One day an earthquake comes and all of it will be gone. Babylon thought it was permanent. Rome thought it was immortal. Concrete? Nothing is concrete in this world. And yet everyone is thrilled to see childish prints in the cement!

"In this rejoice not; but rather rejoice that your names are written in heaven." You do not have to be a star to get your name into that book. The nameless ones get their names there. All followers of Jesus, all who have faith in Him, all who have been born anew, all who are new persons in Christ, shall have their names in the Book of Life.

Do you feel it does not matter whether you are true or false? Faithful or faithless? Virtuous or villainous? It does not even matter whether you live or die? All week long you sit at a bench, a table, a desk. You pack boxes or cap bottles or file papers; you pound typewriters or wash dishes. On Sunday you slide into a back pew and hope no one notices you. What you do with your life does not really matter. You change the world? That's a laugh! The world does not care about you. You die. The world goes on. Only a few turn their heads, then you are forgotten.

So, what can you do? What does it really matter what

you do with your life, whether you live or die? You are so insignificant. Insignificant? So is one atom. You can't even see an atom. But there is enough power in the atoms of a thimbleful of water to drive an ocean liner to Europe and back. You are so inconsequential. Inconsequential? So is one snowflake. So fragile, so light, it would hardly move the most delicate scale. But join one with millions and highways are blocked, locomotives halted, planes grounded, cities brought to a standstill, and a countryside blanketed in white.

You do not count to God? Actually bread is more valuable than diamonds. Diamonds may cost more, but you can't eat them. Water is more precious than pearls. Farmers are more important than movie stars. Maybe that does not come out in the headlines, but, of course, it is so. God's biggest problem is not with the important people. There are only a few of them, really. God's biggest problem is with you and me. We think that what we are, and what we do, is not important after all. But in a story about talented people—one had five, another two, another one—Jesus threw the spotlight on the one-talent man. He had hidden his talent. He thought he was unimportant, inconsequential—and so he was judged.

All heaven wonders what kind of a person you are going to be, what you are going to do with your important life! Will you be true or false, faithful or faithless? How do I know this is so? You see, there stands a Cross. That Cross tells you how much you mean to God. It tells you Jesus came and died for *you*. It expresses the love of God. James, the less—apostle unknown—is a symbol of millions of nobodies. Nobodies? Somebodies! Persons for whom Christ died, children of God, citizens of the Kingdom, whose names are recorded in the Book of Life.

* * * * * * * * * * * * *

Only questions can be raised about Simon, the Zealous Apostle, and James, the Unknown Apostle. Where did Simon preach Christ? Did he die a martyr? Was he crucified? Supposedly.

Did James preach in Israel? In Egypt? Or both? Was he crucified? Supposedly. The sources are most unauthentic. Next to nothing is known of either of these men.

But is that not consistent? Are they not completely in the background? Of neither do we hear anything in Scripture; we can only conjecture. Why, therefore, would the picture change during early Church history? Simon and James remain the saints of the nameless ones, yet named by the Saviour and known *by name* to God!

7

Judas, the Steady Apostle

He Stuck It Out

If a man love me, he will keep my words. And my Father will love him, and we will come unto him and make our abode with him (Jn. 14:23).

A magazine advertisement showed an empty desk chair, comfortable and imposing. Behind the chair a chart pictured an upsurge in business . . . and a black dot with a sharp decline in the chart. At that black dot to explain the empty executive chair as well as the disastrous chart were the words: "This is when the key man died."

Not only can this happen when the key man dies, but it happens every time a man who is counted on fades out of the picture . . . every time a person with responsibility shrugs off that responsibility and leaves—every time a Christian quits. And that happens all too often. Many walk in the company of Jesus, and then for some strange reason they have had enough.

One of the apostles is particularly noted for his steadfastness. There is some confusion about him. In Matthew he is called: "Lebbaeus, whose surname was Thaddaeus." In Mark he is called: "Thaddaeus." In Luke and John he is called: "Judas, the brother of James."

He is the same man since he appears in the same position in the listing of the twelve, and is named in connection with James II. After the betrayal of Jesus, a terrible stigma was upon the name "Judas" and so, perhaps, it was dropped by Matthew and Mark. Luke and John, however, call him Judas (properly, Judas Thaddaeus, over against Judas Iscariot) and we will call him that.

Now this Judas Thaddaeus is the steady apostle. Why? One Judas turned traitor, quit, sold Jesus to His enemies. The other Judas did not quit. He did not turn traitor. He remained steadfast, constant. That in itself is enough of a reason to call him the steadfast apostle.

There is another reason: One incident in the gospel of John puts the spotlight on this Judas. It is the only time he comes to the fore. It is the only incident from which we can tell his personality.

Do we know what we mean by "steadfastness"? "Stead" means a place, a spot. (The old homestead, we say.) "Fast" means fast in place, firmly fixed. To be steadfast is to remain constant, to endure, to be firmly established, not to quit. The steadfast person does not fade out of the picture. He is dependable, sturdy and fixed in purpose.

Once, and only once, Judas asks a question recorded in the gospels. The scene: the Last Supper. The hour: after supper. The occasion: Jesus' last instructions to his men. The problem: how to convey the future to the disciples. The new teaching: after his resurrection, Jesus will send the Holy Spirit and be with them, not in person, but in spirit, not physically, yet in reality!

Judas has been listening. For three years he has trudged along steadily. He has been faithful, dependable, the silent ever-willing workman. Now if there is to be a change, his slow mind wants to make sure what it will be. He must understand before he can swing his solid frame behind it. How will this change be effected? What will it mean to them that Jesus is "gone"? How will they know Him?

"Then Judas (not Iscariot) said, "Lord, how is it that you are going to make yourself known to us but not to the world?" (Jn. 14:22, *Phillips*).

How can a question like that be answered? What do you say? How can you explain to a child how electricity works? How can scientists explain to the public how to get a satellite into orbit? How then can we possibly grasp how God will show Himself to us?

Jesus did not try to explain "how." All He said was: You must do this, and then that will be so . . . "When a man loves me, he follows my teaching. Then my Father will love him, and we will come to that man and make our home within him" (Jn. 14:23, *Phillips*).

Nothing new is said, because nothing new can be said intelligibly. "Because of your love for Me, you will keep my words. Because of God's love for you, We, the Father and Son, will come to you." The pure in heart shall see God!

What is this but an answer encouraging steadfastness! You have loved me, keep on loving me. You have kept my words, keep on doing my words. As you keep on, fixed in purpose, persevering in faith, not quitting, the Father and the Son will make their home in your heart.

The Bible speaks much about steadfastness. It is the main point of the letter of Jude, written by the namesake of this steady apostle. That letter is written to Christians. It says: Do not go astray. Do not be overcome by false teachers. Do not be moved away from the gospel. Hold steadfast to the "faith which was once delivered unto the saints." Earnestly contend for the faith. "Remember ye the words which were spoken before by the apostles of our Lord Jesus Christ; building up yourselves on your most holy faith . . . . Keep yourselves in the love of God" (Jude vs. 3,17,20,21).

We agree on the importance of steadfastness, though how does one continue steadfastly? What is the secret? How can we do it? How can we be like this apostle, steadfast in the faith?

"When a man loves Me, he follows My teaching. Then My Father will love him, and We will come to that man and make Our home within him." We must fulfill the condition. Everything hinges on, "When a man loves me . . . . " When a man —any man—observes the conditions, he may have—will have—the presence of Christ! To "love God" needs to be our desire. Steadfastness implies desiring it over and over again. The weekly habit of worship encourages steadfastness. The constant habit of devotions keeps one steadfast.

"The secret of success is constancy of purpose," said Disraeli. If you do not desire to resist the devil, you will not resist him. If you do not seek to endure to the end, you will meet failure. If you do not desire to love God, you will stop short. It is easy to quit. It is tough to keep going.

In 1815 Wellington was talking to his forces at Waterloo. "Hard pounding this, Gentlemen," he said, "Let's see who can pound the longest." That is the secret. Who can pound the longest? To him go the spoils of victory. How? No easy answer; no new answer, really. Just keep pounding, keep going, fixed in purpose—"Keep yourselves in the love of God."

Or, to put it another way: Keep your eyes on Jesus. Keep your eyes on the object of love. Keep your eyes on the teacher in school, and you will hardly have a desire to cheat. Keep your eyes on your husband or wife, and you will not be unfaithful.

There is a story about Leonardo da Vinci as he painted the picture of "The Last Supper." A crowd watched over his shoulder. He was working on the fruit on the table, and he saw the crowd looking at his every stroke. With one angry brush stroke he obliterated the fruit and pointing to the face of Christ, said: "Don't look down there; look up here." "When a man loves Me, he follows My teaching."

The Westminster Confession of Faith contains a masterful definition of steadfastness: "This perseverance of the saints depends not upon their own free will, but upon election, flowing from the free and unchangeable love of God the Father . . . upon the merit and intercession of Jesus Christ; (upon) the abiding of the Spirit; and of the seed of God within them." It depends upon God: the Father, the Son, and the Holy Spirit.

So, our desire to remain steadfast is necessary. But it can never be enough. God alone can keep you from slipping. God alone can help you to remain steadfast. Therefore, Jude says: "Keep yourselves in the love of God." Then he adds: "Now unto him that is able to keep you from falling . . . the only wise God . . . " (Jude, vs. 21,24,25).

Rely upon God. As you rely on the electric company to provide you with electricity—as you rely on the gas company to provide you with gas—as you rely on the telephone company every time you pick up your phone—so rely on God. Rely on the power of God. Trust. Expect. Be confident. Believe in His presence.

That was Jesus' message to Judas. That was His answer for steadfastness. And, if we can say nothing else about Judas, we can say that he did remain steadfast. He proclaimed Christ faithfully. Toward the end of his life he is said to have preached in the regions of Edessa, Armenia and Persia. Some say he met a martyr's death in Persia. He remained steadfast to the very end.

There is a marker on the rock near the top of Mt. Washington. It marks the spot where a woman climber lay down and died. She was so close to the top that you can almost hit it with a stone. A hundred steps more and she would have reached the hut, the shelter she sought. But she did not know this. She was disheartened by the storm. She was beaten in body, distressed in spirit, at the end of her courage. She could not see a step ahead. She could not measure how far she had to go. She died one hundred steps from her goal!

No, you cannot do everything, but you can keep going. You can take one step more! Even when you think you've reached the end of the line, when you think everything is spent, you can take one step more. Judas Thaddaeus kept his eyes on Christ. He knew the power of Christ to the end of his days. And he treasured the words spoken so personally to him (and to you, also!): "When a man loves Me, he follows My teaching. Then my Father will love him, and we will come to that man and make our home within him."

8

Judas, the Traitor

The Traitor

One of you shall betray me. Then the disciples looked one on another, doubting of whom he spake (Jn. 13:21,22).

I have a standing quarrel with the common characterization of Judas. He is always dressed in black, in contrast to Jesus' white. He is always lurking in the shadows, face twisted in anger, menacing eyebrows, hair unruly, as if he had just stepped from a photo in the police files.

That's convenient, of course. It makes Judas a treacherous gangster, a dirty hoodlum with whom we have nothing to do. In reality you may brush shoulders with him in any crowd; you may be doing business with him daily. He may even be sitting next to you in church! He was an apostle.

Some preachers may be to blame for this picture. I have the highest respect for Dr. G. Campbell Morgan, the late great English expositor, but I take issue with his statement, when he says: "I do not believe that Judas was a man in the ordinary sense of the word; he was a devil incarnate, created in history for the nefarious work that was hell's work." That picture of Judas does not appear in Scripture.

This is not to say that I want to whitewash Judas. There have been many such attempts. One of the first was by De Quincy, over one hundred years ago; one of the latest is by the fine Greek writer, Kazantzakis. Judas is turned from villain to hero. Some make him a loyal disciple who felt called upon to turn Jesus over to the authorities so that He would declare himself as Messiah.

The truth is that Judas is somewhere between a devil and a saint, somewhere between a black-cloaked villain and a white-washed hero. He is a man! One of the best summations of the traitor Judas comes from the pen of Dorothy Sayers: "One thing is certain: He cannot have been the creeping, crawling, patently worthless villain that some simple-minded people would like to make out; that would be to cast too grave a slur upon the brains or the character of Jesus. To choose an obvious crook as one's follower . . . would be the act of a fool; and Jesus of Nazareth was no fool."*

Let us see what the Scripture says about Judas. Let us form our opinions from Scripture: "And it came to pass in those days, that he [Jesus] went out into a mountain to pray, and continued all night in prayer to God. And when it was day, he called unto him his disciples: and of them he chose twelve, whom also he named apostles: . . . Judas Iscariot" (Lk. 6:12-16).

* Op. cit., p. 30.

All night in prayer . . . the apostles chosen—Judas! This then is clear: Judas was chosen as an apostle. He was not chosen to betray Jesus. He was not chosen to become a traitor. Judas had the same chances as Peter and James and John and Philip and Nathanael. He was dressed the same as they. He looked the same as they. He heard what they heard. He saw what they saw. He proclaimed the kingdom message. He went out witnessing as they did. For three years he was an apostle of Jesus Christ. For three years he was in close company with our Lord.

Do not relegate him to the police files! There must have been something about him for Jesus to choose him— perhaps leadership ability, perhaps intelligence. The fact is that Judas was the only man from the South. All the others were from Galilee. Judas, from Kerioth, came from the region of Judea. What was there about him to make him especially qualify among all the Galileans?

Dante places Judas in the lowest hell. But this means that he could have reached to the highest heaven. He who has one talent can only lose one. He who has ten can lose all ten. The worst is the corruption of the best!

Judas himself showed an eagerness to follow Christ. He wanted to be an apostle. He was eager to follow Jesus. He was ready and willing to forsake all. So Jesus said unto him: "Follow me." And he arose and followed, leaving all gladly.

But notice one thing here. The man from Kerioth, the only man from the South, may have felt strange from the start. They spoke with a Galilean accent. He sounded like a gentleman from the deep South among a group of eleven Bostonians. He may have felt out of place. Was he jealous? Jealous because he did not really belong? I do not think the others meaningfully excluded him. But it is natural to pal with your friends—especially since James and John, Peter and Andrew had been in the fishing business together—especially since Philip and Nathanael had been friends before.

Yes, they elected him treasurer. They respected his gifts and his ability. They had confidence in him, but there was an inner circle, too, a sort of "executive committee" of James and Peter and John; and he as the treasurer was not on the "committee"! Can jealousy and resentment find their breeding ground here?

Judas does not formidably appear in Scripture until his act of betrayal. That was after three years in the company of Jesus. Yet there are two short references before that act, and in these two references we get an insight into his character. No one becomes a traitor all at once! A villain is not made overnight. There are always steps, steps that lead to disaster!

A crowd that had been following Jesus, left Him. The teaching had become difficult and they were offended. "So Jesus asked the Twelve, 'Do you also want to leave me?' Simon Peter answered him, 'Lord, to whom shall we go? Your words are words of eternal life. We have faith, and we know that you are the Holy One of God.' Jesus answered, 'Have I not chosen you, all twelve? Yet one of you is a devil' (Jn. 6:67-70, *NEB*).

Jesus knew then what was going on in Judas. How did He know? The Scripture had prophesied that one should betray Him. But why Judas? How did He know it was Judas? He could see it. There were already signs (as there are always signs): uneasiness at the preaching services, stubbornness, prayerlessness, quarrelsomeness in the fellowship, little jealousies, resentments, remarks with double meaning, pride in spiritual growth, showing off one's spiritual muscles.

Jesus can tell, but Judas does not know! Judas himself does not think so. All is well with him. He is enjoying his religion. He is happy in service. He is an apostle, a follower; he is growing! Traitor? Villain? That was the furthest thing from his mind. Had you asked him then, he would have laughed in your face: "Me betray Jesus? You must be crazy! Never! Why the Man is great. He is the Messiah, the Son of God. Why should I betray Him?"

The next step to disaster is just before Palm Sunday. We are only a few days from the act of betrayal. The lies are forming. Still Judas is unaware of the turn his character had taken. He cannot see himself as he really is. Jesus sat at supper in the house of Mary, Martha, and Lazarus. After supper Mary took a costly box of perfumed oil. She poured it out and wiped Jesus' feet. The heavenly fragrance filled the room.

Hers was an act of devotion, but Judas objected: "Why was this perfume not sold for thirty pounds* and given to the poor?" (Jn. 12:5, *NEB*). He was not alone in his reaction. The other disciples also considered it a waste. So, Judas is not the black-cloaked villain we make him out to be, when the gospels make it clear that the others felt exactly as he did.

Only in later years looking back on the episode, John adds: "He said this, not out of any care for the poor, but because he was a thief; he used to pilfer the money put into the common purse, which was in his charge" (Jn. 12:6, *NEB*). The others did not know he was a thief at the time. John found out later, when they audited the books.

* $100.00

So the character is sketched: Judas, like many a follower of Jesus, is a man of double motives. Expressing concern for the poor, his true motive is covetousness. Showing outward acts of piety, his inner desire is avarice, greed under the cloak of good works. A person who says the right word, but does the wrong deed, or no deed at all . . . a person who serves self in the place of Christ. "He followed Christ and yet took his sin with him. Thence . . . his ruin!"*

And now, the act of betrayal: "Then Satan entered into Judas Iscariot, who was one of the Twelve; and Judas went to the chief priests and officers of the temple police to discuss ways and means of putting Jesus into their power. They were greatly pleased and undertook to pay him a sum of money. He agreed, and began to look out for an opportunity to betray him to them without collecting a crowd" (Lk. 22:3-6, *NEB*). The big question: Why did he do it? Why did he turn informer? Why did he hurt Jesus?

All the theories must cope with the Scriptural explanation: "Then Satan entered into Judas." Not unwillingly, of course. Judas opened the door. Judas had taken steps, steps to disaster, and the door swung closed to Jesus!

The scene of betrayal is of all places the Communion Table. It all began with that terrible act of humility. Jesus washed the feet of the disciples. With a towel and basin, He moved on hands and knees from one speechless disciple to another. To Judas, also! Judas' feet! Judas sat there tense, uncomfortable, contemplating his treachery. There was nothing to do, but accept it. Jesus washed Judas' feet, looked at him silently, tried to win him, appealed to his conscience. It only hardened Judas. He froze.

* Marcus Dods. *The Gospel of St. John,* Vol. II, p. 105, Funk & Wagnalls, 1900.

They sit around the Table now. Jesus is about to insti-
tute the Last Supper. But He cannot go through with it;
not with Judas there. Troubled in spirit, He drops the
bombshell: "One of you shall betray me" (Jn. 13:21). No
one points to Judas and asks: "Is it he?" No one even looks
at Judas. He is above suspicion. He is a high caliber, loyal
disciple.

Instead, each one points to himself: One of us? Which
one? "Is it I, Lord?" "Is it I?" (Mt. 26:22). They are full of
questions, deeply disturbed. Finally the one who it is asks
the question also: "Am I the one?" And Jesus replies: "As
you say" (Mt. 26:25, *Phillips*).

Even then Jesus offers him a morsel out of the common dish—a gesture of friendship. Judas receives it, but it
is too much. He gets to his feet, bolts out of the room,
slams the door. "Now no man at the table knew . . . " (Jn.
13:28). They do not suspect him even now. They think he
has gone out to take care of some financial matters. He
goes out into the dark—into the night— alone, forever
alone!

Everything was waiting for him. The Roman contin-
gent had formed. The soldiers in their short, pleated
tunics were ready. The priests expected him. They called
the guards. He led them down the hill, through the city
gate, down through the valley of Kidron, across the brook,
and up the slope toward the garden of Gethsemane.

He had told them: "The one I kiss will be the man. Get
him!" (Mt. 26:48, *Phillips*). Betrayal with a kiss! Judas
could have told them where to go, where to find Jesus.
But no, he will go himself and point out Jesus with a kiss of
betrayal. Not for thirty pieces of silver, but for *revenge:*
resentment, hatred, jealousy, frustration, wounded pride!

Amid the group of trees, Judas spots a white garment.

He motions the soldiers to stop, and steps forward alone
. . . "Greetings, Master!" (Mt. 26:49, *Phillips*). And as he
kisses the Master, one more appeal—the very last
appeal—comes from Jesus' lips: "My friend, (FRIEND!)
what made you come here?" (Mt. 26:50, *Phillips*). But it
is far too late. Judas has a closed mind. The soldiers
advance. They take Jesus, and lead Him away. "So now
you have betrayed Him, Judas! Yet in so doing you have
done something almost as bad. Judas, you have betrayed
yourself!"

That is not the end of the story. The traitor sees Jesus
that very night, accused, tried, and found guilty. The next
morning he will have remorse! A surge of guilt courses
through him. A lonely bitterness boils within him. A vol-
cano of tormented memories—he has betrayed innocent
blood!

This baffles us, does it not? How could he betray
Jesus? That is one question. Why did he have such
remorse? That is another. Surely this is part of the explanation: Judas is not a hardened criminal—a ruthless,
remorseless degenerate. He is a man sensitive to the
promptings of the Spirit! He has been influenced by the
teaching of Jesus. He has a tender conscience. He cannot
help but feel a measure of guilt.

If there was any avarice, any greed, or any covetousness, that all passes out of the picture too. He runs back to
the temple. He makes his confession: "I have sinned! I
have sinned! I have betrayed innocent blood." (See Mt.
27:4.) He opens his money-bag, grabs out the thirty
pieces of silver and throws them violently on the temple
floor. Now rid of the blood-money, he leaves the city.

Out on a nearby cliff, he knows the place well, stands a

tree. One branch hangs over the edge . . . He approaches that tree, throws a rope over the low-hanging limb. He fastens it securely, then ties the other end into a slip-knot. His hands shake as he places the knot over his head. One final look around, the perspiration stands cold on his forehead. He throws his body over the cliff . . . the line snaps taut.

And the words spoken by the Lord find their fulfillment in the suicide of the traitor: "The Son of Man is going the way appointed for him in the scriptures; but alas for that man by whom the Son of Man is betrayed! It would be better for that man if he had never been born" (Mt. 26:24, *NEB*).

Scripture gives one final word about Judas: "Judas by transgression fell, that he might go to his own place" (Acts 1:25). We cannot read that without pain. What could have been his! Chosen as an apostle, chosen to the highest, chosen for the Kingdom of God, chosen by Jesus who said: "I go to prepare a place for you . . . " (Jn. 14:2). But he went to his own place. He chose that place himself.

But, how could anyone who lived in the presence of Jesus for three years do this? How could anyone be so near to Jesus, and fall so far away? *That is his message to us!* One could, and one did. He who professes allegiance to the Church who, when a chance for worldly advancement arises, turns his back, is a traitor too! You and I, we are of like passions with Judas.

Jesus had much to say to Judas . . . much, every day. And Judas heard, but he did not hear. The warnings, the pleadings, the word of God reached him, but it never really reached him. He turned traitor to himself in spite of Jesus' appeals.

*And what of us? You and me? We hear Jesus speak.
We know what we ought to do. Do we let Him
change us? Do we think we are all right, and go on
calling Him, "Lord, Lord," but do not the things
which He says? That was the only trouble with
Judas! Shall we not then examine our own hearts?
When Jesus says: "One of you shall betray Me,"
shall we not join the other disciples, and ask: "Lord,
is it I?"*

* * * * * * * * * * * * *

"I have done a thing so hideous that hell itself
is ashamed! The vilest thieves have some loyalty,
and a scoundrel's dog can be faithful to him. But
my Master was innocent, and I slandered him;
innocent, and I accused him; innocent, and I
betrayed him.

"It was written that He must suffer—Yes! And
why? Because there are too many men in the
world like me . . . I wanted to believe him guilty,
because I could not endure his innocence . . . Do
you know what hell-fire is? It is the light of God's
unbearable innocence that sears and shrivels you
like flame. It shows you what you are. It is a fear-
ful thing to see one's self for a moment as one
really is.

"Is God merciful? Can He forgive? . . . What
help is that? . . . Can anything clear me . . . ? Or

release me from this horror . . . ? What shall I do?
. . . What shall I do? I am unclean! . . . Unclean
and accurst . . . Unclean . . . Accurst . . . " *

*Dorothy Sayers. op.ct., 275,276.

9

Peter, the Magnificent Apostle

From Sand to Rock

*Depart from me, for I am a sinful man, O Lord
(Lk. 5:8). Lord, to whom shall we go? Thou hast
the words of eternal life (Jn. 6:68). Lord, Thou
knowest that I love Thee . . . (Jn. 21: 16).*

Anything you want to say about him, any word of
praise, any descriptive adjective, any commendation will
fit. Call him wonderful if you wish—superb—
phenomenal—amazing—great—even Hollywood will run
out of adjectives to describe him. It is all true for the foremost of the twelve for the big Galilean fisherman, for
Peter, the magnificent.

Now we have said enough about other apostles to
show that they were ordinary men. They had few talents.
Some had little ability. Andrew, Peter's brother, had but
one talent, but he learned to play second fiddle well. Judas
Thaddaeus hardly opened his mouth. He just plodded

along. James, the less, is completely obscure, totally unknown. But what they lacked, Peter had. For every talent they possessed, he had ten. He was that kind of a man.

Someone had to be a leader among the twelve, and he was the one. He had always been a leader. He was born that way. He probably went deepest into the caves, swam farthest in the Sea of Galilee, and climbed the highest mountains. He dominated every fishing expedition. He gave the orders.

So as an apostle, he dominates the gospel narratives. He is the first to speak, the first to act. He is impulsive and impetuous, tempestuous and talented, enthusiastic, extreme, an extrovert. He is, as named by Jesus Christ, "the Rock": "I tell you that you are Peter, the rock" (Mt. 16:18, *Phillips*).

But that road to becoming "the Rock"—the road that leads to stability, to firmness, to strength, to granite purpose is no easy road. It is the straight and narrow, and it is beautifully etched for us in the gospels. With this in mind let us look at Peter, the magnificent apostle, and we shall see what made him so magnificent—what made him "the Rock."

Despite all his gifts, Peter was a humble man. With all his brash bravado, he was sensitive, penetrative. He had a tender conscience. He knew his own heart!

This is what makes him great. He did not adulterate his gifts for himself. He knew his inadequacy; he knew himself. In this light he appears in Scripture right from the start.

They had been fishing all night. They had caught nothing. They came in tired. Jesus stood by the Sea of Galilee and said to Simon: "Put out into deep water and let down your nets for a catch" (Lk. 5:4-10, *NEB*). Of course he objected: "Master, we were hard at work all night and caught nothing at all; [and then he sighed and changed his mind] but if you say so, I will let down the nets." Out they went, after the night of failure, and what a catch! The fish filled the net so that it broke!

Now Andrew was not impenitent, and John was deeply sensitive. But Peter, seeing the miracle, comes off the boat running, falls on his knees at Jesus feet, and cries out: "Go Lord, leave me, sinner that I am!" He cannot bear it. That impulsive, sudden penitence—that humility that tender conscience marks Peter as the captain of the new fishing fleet, as the leader of the twelve: "Do not be afraid . . . from now on you will be catching men."

So it was all through his life—genuine humility. The Lord could reach Peter; He gives grace only to the humble. The difference between Peter and Judas is just here: both denied Jesus; but Peter has the humility that will save him from despair. Judas has no humility, hence his despair leads to his downfall.

Once, much later, he was rebuked by the apostle Paul. Paul withstood Peter to the face, pointed out how Peter had reversed himself, how he had wobbled and caused confusion to Christians. Peter took it like a man. He knew he was wrong. He did not defend himself.

Toward the end of his life, Peter wrote a letter revealing his still tender conscience: "Add to your faith, virtue, knowledge, temperance, godliness, love. The man who lacks them is short-sighted and blind; he has forgotten how he was cleansed from his former sins" (II Pet. 1:5,9, *NEB*). The man who remains humbled by his sins is on the way to stability. This is the road to "the Rock."

Failure—often blinding failure—was his lot. When not

inspired he can plunge into bad blunders. One of our comedians had an oft-repeated line after he had put his foot in it. He knew he had blundered, and there is no way out; so he could only say: "Me and my big mouth." That was Peter, rash, unthinking, impulsive. Time and again he probably said to himself: "Me and my big mouth."

Take that time the disciples found themselves in the turbulence of a storm at sea. Suddenly it seemed as if they saw a ghost walking on the water toward them. Even Peter felt a turn in the pit of his stomach, and he cried out afraid!

A voice answered them (from the "ghost"): "Take heart! It is I; do not be afraid" (Mt. 14:27-30, *NEB*). It was their Lord, Jesus Christ. Peter could not believe it. But now foolhardy, daring, he must do what Jesus is doing! If it is He, then Peter must walk on the water, too: "Lord, if it is you, tell me to come to you over the water." The Lord said, "Come," and Peter went over the side impulsively, blindly.

Suddenly he woke up to what he was doing. Walking on the water? Ridiculous! Unheard of! That does not make sense. In his fear he started to sink: "Save me, Lord." Jesus was right there, lifted him up and took him back aboard ship.

Peter with his impetuous speech did make that great confession. Jesus had asked them a vital question: "And you, who do you say I am?" (Mt. 16:15-23, *NEB*). Explosive, quick to reply, Peter was the one to speak up: "You are the Messiah, the Son of the living God."

Jesus made it clear that this insight had not come from Peter himself but from God: "You did not learn that from mortal man; it was revealed to you by my heavenly Father." And then he added: "You are Peter, the Rock;

and on this rock I will build my church, and the forces of death shall never overpower it."

No sooner had He said it and "the Rock" disintegrated. Jesus began to show the apostles (for the first time) how He must suffer, be persecuted, and killed. Peter could not believe it. He took Him aside: "No, Lord, this shall never happen to you." And the Lord rebuked him severely: "Away with you, Satan; you are a stumbling-block to me. You think as men think not as God thinks." One moment inspired by God; the next the tool of the devil. Many a failure and many a stumble before Peter could become granite rock!

Of course he really put his foot in it after the Lord's Supper. He had been in the presence of Jesus for three years, and he has begun to think of himself as "the Rock"—sure, strong, steady, faithful. Nothing can ever move him again. He is the leader of the twelve.

So Peter is deeply shocked when Jesus starts quoting Scripture: "You will all fall from your faith; for it stands written: 'I will smite the shepherd and the sheep will be scattered abroad'" (Mk. 14:27-31, *Phillips*).

Peter challenges Him. "Everyone else may fall away, but I will not." He will never deny Jesus. Whatever else he may be, he is not a deserter.

Since he had spoken up, Jesus turned to Peter and said quietly, but firmly: "I tell you this: today, this very night, before the cock crows twice, you yourself will disown me three times." That infuriated him. He meant what he said, and now he would say it again: "Even if I must die with you, I will never disown you." The rock would not fail.

That night after they took Jesus, His followers forsook Him. Peter followed into the court-square. Afterwards he wished that he had not gone in. But he did go. He ventured further than his courage would carry him. And so he was caught off guard by a sudden question. Then he started down that fatal slope, unable to stop himself, going down faster and faster—until finally, too late, came that terrible awakening and that bitter sense of shame!

He warmed himself by the fire. It was cold that night. He was already excited, nervous, upset, and it felt good to warm himself. A group stood around joking, talking and discussing the latest events in Jerusalem.

A servant girl in the group—she may have seen him somewhere before—looked at him strangely and asked: "You were there too, with this man from Nazareth, this Jesus" (Mk. 14:67-72, *NEB*). He muttered in his beard, so hardly anyone could hear: "I know nothing. I do not understand what you mean." And the sweat stood out on his forehead. He realized what he was saying.

He felt the eyes of the group on him. They were talking about him and he knew it. He kept his eyes down—into the fire. But another girl came around to where he stood and turned to him: "He is one of them," she said to her companions. Peter talked a little louder than before. They could all hear now, as he denied again!

"The Rock"? He spoke so courageously. He would never deny Him. And now . . . ?

Then that soldier joined the group. Perhaps one of the soldiers who had taken Jesus in the garden. He looks at Peter, and Peter feels the blood rush to his head. Then he says it: "He is one of them." And someone else says: "Surely you are one of them. You must be; you are a Galilean."

Then he swears and curses, using language he has not used in years, and they all stand quiet before his vehemence: *"I do not know this man you speak of."* And then, in that moment of quiet, he can hear it, loud and clear—like a bugle call—the crowing of the cock! And he remembers: "Before the cock crows twice, you will disown me three times."

And then, then just at that moment, the Lord appears. At the top of the stairs, condemned, tried, to be led to Pilate's judgment hall, and He looks straight down. And all eyes look up, and Peter looks up, and their eyes meet. He knows! That was too much for Peter! He bit his lip. His tears started coming. And he rushed out of the court-square, out of the gate, out . . . his heart pounding, his emotions throbbing. He had collapsed like rotten timber. "The Rock" had turned to sand . . . !

Something happened to Peter that night, something tremendous, something that became for him a turning point, a conversion if you like. Something died within him. Something was killed: his cocksure confidence—his brash bravado—his self-reliance—his strength in himself. He was "the Rock"? That Rock would never be moved? Nonsense—he was sand—and he knew it.

Could he ever be forgiven for this? He remembered how Jesus had said that a man should forgive seventy times seven. But could he ever forgive himself? He could not sleep. He could not eat. He took his failure hard.

Then broke that glorious news of Easter. They rushed to the empty tomb. They listened to the stories. They saw Him. Still Peter nursed his terrible shame.

Finally came that morning by the Sea of Galilee. Peter had led them back to their fishing. Back to the familiar, the old ways, the old life, to forget the recent regrets and the failures. That night they caught nothing.

A Man stood on the shore, and He told them to cast their nets on the right side. They did so, and caught a great school of fish. John cried out: "It is the Lord" (Jn. 21:7-17, *Phillips*). That was enough for Peter. Impetuously he threw himself into the water and swam ashore. The Lord had built a little fire, cooked some fish, and breakfast was ready. There in the early dawn they ate together quietly. Peter did not dare to speak.

After breakfast Jesus broke the silence. With a searching look He turned to Peter: "Simon, son of John, do you love me more than these others?" (He had called him by his given name, not by his new name, Peter "the Rock.") It hurt him, but could he say he loved Him? Could he say it after his denial? "Yes, Lord, you know that I am your friend."

Jesus turned again to Peter with the same question; "Simon, son of John, do you love me?" He had deserted, denied, disowned Him. Could he say that he loved Him? "Yes, Lord, you know that I am your friend."

And a third time Jesus turned and He changed His question: "Simon, son of John, *are* you my friend?" "Lord you know everything. You know that I am your friend." Three times he had denied. Three times the opportunity was given to reaffirm. No condemnation, only the chance to be reinstated as Jesus' friend. This is the grace of God for the humble.

So the command was given: "Feed my sheep." Peter is sent back to Jerusalem, back to the place where he had failed. And Peter is humble enough now, subdued enough now, not to object. He goes and preaches. He uses his gifts to bring thousands into the Kingdom. He faces persecution. He had quailed before the question of a servant girl; he can face a mob unafraid now.

The Rock was beginning to form. Amid all the stumbles and falls (and they continued, for sometimes the sand would show up again) the name the Master had given him would come into reality. His humility, his devotion, his shattered self-assurance, his experience of the Lord's forgiveness, kept bringing him back in love to Jesus Christ.

He followed his Lord wherever He would lead. Even to Rome, to death, to a Cross, for tradition tells us that he felt unworthy to be crucified as his Lord and was crucified upside-down.

By now he knew that

> *"to be called by Christ is a gift*
> *to be overcome by Christ is freedom*
> *to die with Christ is life."**

* * * * * * * * * * * * *

The Acts of the Apostles turns the spotlight on Peter. He preaches the first Christian sermon. He endures persecution, and withstands the authorities. He is the strength of the early Jewish-Christian community and then is led by God's Spirit to reach the Gentiles; he brings the good news to Cornelius, a Roman.

However, during the first Church Council at Jerusalem (recorded in Acts 15), Peter acknowledges the leadership of James. Subsequently he leaves Jerusalem in James' hands and the conversion of the Gentile world to Paul. He appears at Antioch (Gal. 2:11) and Corinth (I Cor. 1:12) but little is told of his travels and labors.

Only through the letters which he wrote do we receive insight into his development and his understanding of the

---

*Edmund Schlinck, *The Victor Speaks*, p. 95, Concordia Pub. House, St. Louis, 1958.

Christian faith. Peter's letters reveal his warmth and sincerity, his faith in times of testing, his reliance upon Christ in suffering and his unfading hope of glory.

According to tradition he died in Rome. How long he resided there prior to his death is not known. The sources are contradictory. His manner of death had been foretold by Jesus: "When you grow old, you will stretch out your hands, and someone else will gird you, and bring you where you do not wish to go. This He said, signifying by what kind of death he would glorify God" (John 21:18,19, *American Standard Bible*). He was crucified, but whether he was crucified upside down, as tradition tells us, is also debatable.

Perhaps the legend which recounts Peter's arrival in Rome has some truth behind it: He arrived at Rome during heavy persecution. He witnessed Christians being martyred, and he fled. Outside the city he met a man headed for Rome, carrying a cross.

Peter asked him: "Quo Vadis?" (Where are you going?)

The man replied: "To Rome, to be crucified again."

Peter had made his last retreat. He returned to the city—and martyrdom. The Rock was still being formed!

10

James, the Ambitious Apostle

The Ambitious One

Then came to him the mother of Zebedee's children
with her sons . . . desiring a certain thing . . . (Mt.
20:20).

They all had mothers; of course they had. And the
character of one such mother is vividly sketched in Scripture. She is the wife of Zebedee, a fisherman. She is the
sister of Mary, probably the mother of Jesus. She is
mother of two apostles, James and John.

On one occasion during the ministry of Jesus she came
to Him with her two sons. She came with a request:
"Grant that these my two sons may sit, the one on thy
right hand, and the other on the left, in thy kingdom" (Mt.
20:21). She asked for the places of honor. My two sons—
prime-minister and vice-president.

I cannot help but ask a few questions about Mrs. Zebedee: Did she run the home? Did she boss her husband?

Did she domineer the household so that everyone jumped at her every call? What did she live for? What did she want out of life? Did she thrust her whole ambition on her family, on her two sons? Did she want everyone to go around saying what a capable, wonderful person she was—what a magnetic, powerful personality she had?

There are some mothers who want to fulfill in their children what they could not fulfill in themselves. They push their children. They drive their children. They want them to be a success, to have honors. They do not seek it for the sake of the child alone. They desire it for themselves. Will not everyone look up to Mrs. Zebedee when James and John, her sons, are the leaders in the Kingdom?

Behind James, the apostle, stood an ambitious mother. But let me say this to her credit: She followed Jesus Christ. She believed in Jesus Christ. And she changed. She was there at the Cross when He died. Jesus did not gain a throne. He gained a Cross, and she was there.

The ambition of the mother rubbed off on the son. This is more true for James than for his brother John, who also was brought up in this tension-filled home. Though John was temperamental, there was something gentle and sensitive and loving about him. Ambition could not take hold of him as it could James. It bounced off his gentle spirit, and then found its way into the heart of James.

James was the older of the two—a fisherman by trade, in business with his father. Nicknamed by Jesus, "son of thunder," he was a man of strong personality, of fiery temperament.

That explains his reaction against the Samaritans. Jesus had set His face toward Jerusalem. He had to pass through Samaria. Hard feelings existed between the Samaritans and the Jews. And when Jesus sent word to a village to make ready for Him and His disciples, the Samaritans refused.

James and John felt very self-righteous. They remembered how the prophet Elijah had called down fire from heaven. In his indignation against these Samaritans, James now suggested a similar course: "Lord, may we call down fire from heaven to burn them up?" (Lk. 9:54, *NEB*). Let us show our authority. Let everyone know that we can bring fire from heaven. That will give us headlines!

Jesus rebuked them: "You do not know to what spirit you belong; for the Son of Man did not come to destroy men's lives but to save them" (See Lk. 9:55,56). So, on they went to another village.

And so we see him again with his ambitious request: "Grant unto us that we may sit, one on thy right hand, and the other on thy left hand, in thy glory" (Mk. 10:37). Now one thing he will learn from Jesus. He will learn that the places of honor in the Kingdom are not bestowed by favoritism but by fitness. "Ye know not what ye ask. Are ye able to drink of the cup that I shall drink of, and to be baptized with the baptism that I am baptized with?" (Mt. 20:22).

Eager to obtain, the ambitious man will promise anything. James does not know, nor does he care what he is promising, when he replies: "We are able" (Mt. 20:22b).

And Jesus answers in words they hardly understand: "Ye shall drink indeed of my cup, and be baptized with the baptism that I am baptized with: but to sit on my right hand, and on my left, is not mine to give, but it shall be given to them for whom it is prepared of my Father" (Mt. 20:23).

Later, James did understand and he must have looked back and breathed many a prayer of thanks. On His right and on His left? Not when that fateful night rolled around, not when their Lord was betrayed, not when they all forsook Him and fled. Not when they took Jesus before the authorities, not when they beat Him with many stripes in Pilate's court, not when they made Him carry the Cross, not when He hung in shame upon His Cross! Not then to be on His right and on His left in His kingdom! No, they were glad the request was not granted. James was not even there at the cross. He could not face it. He was too much of a coward. Yet Jesus had said that James would drink of His cup: "You shall drink of My cup." Not many of us are aware of a cup to drink. We pass our time with a glass, or perhaps we take it straight from the bottle.

What is that cup? The baptism of Jesus—"and be baptized with the baptism I am baptized with . . . "—what is that? The cup is suffering. The cup is agony. The cup is hardship. The cup is trial. The baptism is identification with men. The baptism is cleansing. The baptism leads to a Cross. The cup is a lot in life, a destiny, the fulfillment of divine purpose.

"We are able." "We will drink it!" Do we know what we say? Do we know what we affirm when we become disciples? Do we know what we mean when we follow Jesus? He who will follow Jesus must bear His cross too.

James came to taste of that cup. He was to become a martyr. In fact, he became the first apostle to give his life. He was killed by the sword of Herod. So he drank of that same cup, and was baptized with the same baptism!

And now we find a little vignette in our story that makes us want to erase the word "saint" from in front of the names of St. Matthew, St. Andrew, and St. Peter. "When the ten heard it"—heard of the ambitious request of James and John, heard how they wanted the places of honor—"When the ten heard it, they were moved with indignation against the two brethren" (Mt. 20:24).

They were jealous. To be more specific, they were ambitious, too! Just as ambitious, only they did not have the courage of the sons of thunder to ask.

Disappointing, isn't it? Their haloes are slipping. We thought them such saints, these twelve. We thought them such heroes. They changed the world. They moved mountains. We placed them on such pedestals. And now—of all things—they resemble us! They are imperfect, selfish, ambitious. Why, they are hypocrites!

And yet this is the point: Jesus used these men. They did change the world. They did move mountains. He did not use perfect men. He did not use polished men. He used these envious, selfish, craving, aspiring men, even James, the most ambitious of them all. He used them because He changed them. How?

By His life. They saw it in His example, when He stooped to wash their feet. "And whosoever will be chief among you, let him be your servant" (Mt. 20:27).

By His death. They knew what He had lived for, what He had taught. Now He demonstrated His teaching. He, the Lord, gave Himself in humiliation. He submitted unto death, even the death of the Cross. "The Son of man came . . . to give his life a ransom for many" (Mt. 20:28).

And *by His Spirit.* A *new* Spirit—not the old selfish ambitions, not the old jealousies and tempers, but the Spirit of God, the Holy Spirit, within them, changing their lives!

Our idea of success is a pyramid. We reach up and up until we can get to the top. The higher we climb, the fewer equals we have, but the more subordinates. And at the apex, at the very top, ambition is reached—success achieved. That was James. He looked for the places at the right and left of Jesus, only the Lord above him, everyone else beneath Him.

Jesus showed him a new ambition: not a pyramid, but an inverted pyramid. The more selfish one is, the nearer one is to the bottom. The higher we climb, the wider will be our range of vision, the greater our service, the more equals we will have. (For remember, the pyramid is upside down). Until He, Jesus, at the very top of love's inverted pyramid, carries the sins of the whole world! "The Son of Man came . . . to give His life a ransom for many."

And so we must decide for our own ambitions to be fulfilled, or for His to be fulfilled in us, to drink our "glass" or to drink His "cup."

There shall always be the Church and the world,
And the heart of man shivering and fluttering
between them. Choosing and chosen . . . Swinging
*between hell gate and heaven gate.**

*   *   *   *   *   *   *   *   *   *   *   *   *

We know what happened to James. Scripture records his untimely death.

King Herod was upon the throne. This Herod was the brother of Herodias, who had been responsible for the beheading of John the Baptist. King Herod imprisoned

* T.S. Eliot, from *Masterpieces of Religious Verse,* "There Shall Always Be the Church," p. 492, James Dalton Morrison, Harper & Row, 1948.

Peter and beheaded James, who was slain by the sword in Jerusalem in the year 44. (See Acts 12:2.)

James was the first apostle to give his life for the faith. He realized his ambition prematurely. He drank of that bitter cup and joined Jesus in His Kingdom.

11

John, the Apostle of Love

From Temper to Tenderness

A new commandment I give unto you, That ye love one another; as I have loved you, that ye also love one another (Jn. 13:34).

If you want theology, read Paul. If you want ethics, read James. But if you want to know about love, if you want the heart of Christianity, you must read John. Of all the twelve apostles there were three who seemed to form an inner circle: James, Peter, and John. And of these three, one came the closest to Jesus: John, the beloved, the disciple whom Jesus loved. Out of that inner communion, out of that close fellowship, out of that heart-to-heart relationship, came a beautiful life, a sensitive spirit, an apostle of love.

Of course this raises a question. Did not Jesus love all the disciples? Of course! Did He not care for *all* men? Of course! Does He not love the world? "God so loved the world, that he gave . . . " (Jn. 3:16). Then why single out John? Then why call him, "the disciple whom Jesus loved?" (See Jn.13:23). Because the love for all does not preclude a special love for some. Jesus wept at the grave of Lazarus. Jesus submitted his mother, at his death, to the care of John.

John came a long way! He was not born with a loving heart, nor was he reborn with it. Some find it easier to love than others, but all of us know that truly to love someone else is something that must grow in life. To love the unlovely, to keep on loving, to love unselfishly, this is a gift of God.

John had a sensitive, gentle spirit, but he was also capable of anger, flare-ups, outbursts. He had a temper. He was excitable, impulsive. He could go for a while but then he would lose control; and like a sudden storm that rises out of nowhere and disappears again before you know it, John could blow up. He won control over that temper. He grew in love and understanding. There is no question about it—he came a long way!

By trade he was a fisherman. His father was a fisherman before him. He grew up in the business. It was prosperous. His father could afford hired servants. But John was restless.

And so when he heard of a prophet in the wilderness, a man who was baptizing in the region round about the Jordan, he asked his father for some time off to hear him. He and Andrew, a friend and also a fisherman, went to hear the Baptist preach. To this sensitive young man it was a stirring sight to see men go down into the River Jordan to be baptized, to respond to the invitation, to witness repentance and conversion. It was a highlight for him when he heard the Baptist preach: "I do baptize—with water. But somewhere among you stands a Man you do not know. He comes after me, it is true, but I am not fit to undo His sandals! Look, there is the lamb of God who will take away the sin of the world" (Jn. 1:26-29, *Phillips*).

And John turned to see to whom the Baptist pointed. As he did so, he got the shock of his life—his own cousin! Jesus, the son of Joseph and Mary, his aunt and uncle. Jesus, his cousin from Nazareth—the carpenter. Lamb of God? He was so muddled in his mind, so disturbed in his thought, that the next day he went to see Jesus about it. So, you think it was easy for John to believe? You think there was nothing to it? He had known Jesus as his cousin. Perhaps when the family got together in vacation times, and his parents had visited in Nazareth, he had played with his cousin. "The Lamb of God?" Would it be easy to believe that your cousin is of God?

From that first announcement and the subsequent talk with Jesus, and to the very end, John believed. He makes much of that belief. It is a key word in his gospel. Ninety-eight times in twenty-one chapters: believe—believe—believe! He came through it himself. "He knows that he speaks the truth, so that you too may believe" (Jn. 19:35, *NEB*). Jesus loves all men. But He especially loves those who believe in Him. Perhaps this is one reason why John held a special place. If you would know the wonder of being beloved of God, have faith in His Son.

So he began by faith. So he grew in love. In his own gospel he is not called by name. Again and again it is: "The disciple whom Jesus loved." (See Jn. 13:23.) They sat about the table. John was closest to Jesus. From that table he reports the new commandment Jesus gave: "A new commandment I give unto you, That ye love one another; as I have loved you, that ye also love one another" (Jn.

13:34). This is his theme: "Love one another . . . By this shall all men know that you are My disciples, if you have love one to another." (See Jn. 13:35.) This is a man who came a long way. Instead of love in his younger life, he had an enthusiasm that bordered on sectarianism.

One day John had been on a preaching mission, and something he saw disturbed him. He came back to Jesus to report. "Master, we saw a man driving out devils in your name, and as he was not one of us, we tried to stop him. Jesus said, 'Do not stop him; no one who does a work of divine power in my name will be able in the same breath to speak evil of me. For he who is not against us is on our side" (Mk. 9:38-40, *NEB*). John was a long way then from his later advice: "Love one another" (Jn. 13:34).

A sectarian, divisive spirit! We alone are able to cast out demons. We alone are the true disciples. Not the Methodists, not the Episcopalians, not the Lutherans, not the Pentecostals, not the Presbyterians! They do not follow us, so we forbad them.

God is not limited. The Holy Spirit is sovereign. Let us not limit God to our persuasion, or our little group. Jesus judged sectarianism, separationism, divisiveness, exclusiveness when He said: "No one who does a work of divine power in my name will be able in the same breath to speak evil of me. Do not stop him." And John, humble enough to take the rebuke, says it over and over again: "Beloved, let us love one another, for love is of God, and everyone that loveth is born of God, and knoweth God" (I John 4:7).

Do not think of John as a tame, milk-toast sort of man. He was sensitive and gentle of spirit, yes. But he had fire, boldness, courage, temper. Both he and his brother James were nicknamed "sons of thunder" (Mk. 3:17) by Jesus.

To talk about the loving apostle may leave the impression of weakness. Still, consider that none of the others, so far as we know, was at the Cross—only John. How did Jesus feel as He looked from that Cross on the sea of faces below? On the faces of hatred, the faces filled with scorn, the faces of indifferent bystanders, the faces of the curious . . . and then the face of understanding, of compassion, of John. Did it take courage to stand there among his enemies? Did it take dedication to stand there? And love? That is love! That is courageous love!

And so it was that in the midst of His agony, Jesus turned with pain to His mother and to John and said: "Woman, behold thy son! [and then to John] Behold thy mother" (Jn. 19:26,27). From that time on John took the mother of Jesus into his home. She was completely entrusted to him who was the beloved among the twelve.

Following the resurrection of Jesus, the apostles preached in Jerusalem. Persecution broke out. They were forbidden to preach and were put into prison. Peter and John answered: "Whether it be right in the sight of God to hearken unto you more than unto God, judge ye. For we cannot but speak the things which we have seen and heard" (Acts 4:19, 20). They were threatened yet went right on giving witness to the resurrection of Jesus with *great power.* A sensitive, gentle, loving spirit, but not tame: bold, powerful, courageous, strong—this kind of love!

There is a legend about John which is not without foundation. When he was so old he could no longer walk, they carried him bodily from his house to the place of worship. Time and again they would ask him to speak. All he would ever say was: "Little children, love one another." Only that, nothing more. Never anything more. And when one day someone dared ask him why he said nothing else, John replied: "Because this is our Lord's sole commandment. If we fulfill this, nothing more is needed."

What is the secret? How then does a person grow into this love? How does one become beloved of Jesus? Believing in Him? Humble before Him, taking rebuke? Having courage to follow Him, standing up for Him? Yes. But there is a secret to a Christ-like life. There is a way to grow in love.

That secret of growing in love, of becoming a loving person, is not found through the intellect but in the heart. This is not to disparage the intellect. John had an amazing grasp of spiritual truth. John had great spiritual insight. John possessed a gifted mind. John gives to us the mystery of the incarnation. John understands the coming of the Son of God into the world. After all, it is John who writes that magnificent passage: "In the beginning was the Word, and the Word was with God, and the Word was God. And the Word was made flesh, and dwelt among us" (Jn. 1:1,14). This opening of his gospel stands supreme over all literature.

John understands Jesus better than any other disciple. He has that capacity. He feels deeply. He knows how to get close to his Lord. And he knows that this is the secret. He says so: "If we walk in the light, as He is in the light . . . He who says he abides in Him, ought himself also so to walk, even as He walked . . . " (See I Jn. 1:7;2:6). "A new commandment I give unto you, that you love one another" (Jn. 13:34). And all the rest of it on love. But how can you love unless you get close to the *source* of that love? How can you progress and grow unless you get so near to the source that the very life of Jesus spills over into yours?

The secret of growing in love is not found through education, but through experience. This does not disparage education, yet John was not a man of learning. Strange, for he writes about the Word made flesh, but has no rabbinical training. He is described as an "ignorant and unlearned" man.

But growth in love, though aided by education, comes through experience. That is, the experience of the presence of God. This lifted John above the others. This meditation on truth, on God, on Christ, this experience of reality—of His presence. This walk in the light, as He is in the light, is the way to grow in love.

Why have we so little faith? Why have we so little strength? Why have we so little conviction, so little hold on reality? Why have we so little growth in love? We read the New Testament but do not take time to think about it. We pretend to pray, but do not really pray. Think about God, about why you are here, about where you are going, about the meaning of life . . . Think about Jesus Christ, His Cross, His Kingdom, His purpose, and it will all be far more real than your morning paper or your evening TV. John could not rely upon a fine education, but he had a great experience. John could not rely upon a highly developed intellect, but he had a great heart!

"We have heard it; we have seen it with our own eyes; we looked upon it, and felt it with our own hands; and it is of this we tell. Our theme is the word of life. This life was made visible; we have seen it and bear our testimony; we here declare to you the eternal life which dwelt with the Father and was made visible to us. What we have seen and heard we declare to you, so that you and we together may share in a common life, that life which we share with the Father and his Son Jesus Christ" (I Jn. 1:1-3, *NEB*). It is not without foundation that the symbol for John is the eagle. To mount up with wings, to fly ever higher, to live so near to heaven—this is John. And that was a long road for John, the beloved: from temper to tenderness—from anger to adoration—from sectarianism to strength in love.

It is a road you, too, may walk, if only you will get near enough to Jesus.

* * * * * * * * * * * * *

Peter and John were good friends. They discovered the empty tomb together. After the outpouring of God's Spirit, they went to the Temple together. They healed a lame man. They were brought before the Council and suffered imprisonment together. They were sent to Samaria to strengthen the Church. In Jerusalem they were considered pillars of the early Church (Gal. 2:9).

His preaching took John out of Jerusalem to various places in Asia Minor. It is fairly well confirmed that he spent his later years in Ephesus. During these years he wrote the Gospel and letters which are in the New Testament.* Three well-known early Christian leaders sat at his feet: Polycarp, Papias and Ignatius.

The Emperor Domitian banished John to the isle of Patmos. Here he saw visions and received the inspiration to write Revelation (Rev. 1:9). He was set free by the Emperor Nerva (96 A.D.) and returned to Ephesus.

John died a natural death in old age, the last of the apostles to die.

---

* St. John; I, II, III John.

12

Thomas, the Doubting Apostle

Doubting Thomas

Because you have seen me you have found faith.
Happy are they who never saw me and yet have
found faith (Jn. 20:29, *NEB*).

He was beyond question the most pessimistic, the most melancholy, morose, and thereby the most stubborn of the disciples. Peter Marshall calls him the "Palestinian Missourian." He will not believe anything he cannot see. He is so factual, so realistic, that he looks at the world, at suffering, at life until he is a thorough-going pessimist, a brooder. To call him "doubting Thomas" is not quite enough. The mule would be a better symbol: hard to move, stubborn, sullen, morose.

What was he ever doing as an apostle of Jesus? Why was he chosen? I don't know, unless Jesus wants to give all kinds of encouragement to anyone who is mulish and melancholy, to anyone pessimistic by nature and full of doubts. Nevertheless, Tennyson may have the key with those famous lines: "There lives more faith in honest doubt, believe me, than in half the creeds."

We meet Thomas the first time when news comes that a friend, Lazarus, has died. Jesus and the apostles were in a village at least a day removed from the scene. After some time Jesus announced to the twelve that they would go back into Judea. By now the storm had gathered in Judea against Him. During heated debates the leaders had twice attempted to stone Him. He had escaped from their midst, and retired to this village beyond the Jordan.

Thomas saw the danger outlined clearly. There was no escaping it. They had been in one skirmish after another, but Jesus had faced it all courageously, unflinchingly. And yet, Thomas knew, He could be killed, for in fact He had begun speaking about a Cross. So as Jesus announced that He was determined to go back into the thick of it again, Thomas turned to the others and said: "Let us also go, that we may die with him" (Jn. 11:16).

That was devotion, yet that was also the voice of a melancholy soul, gloomy, depressed, ever looking at the dark side of things—ever ready to be a pessimist. He sounded like a man devoid of hope, resigned to fate, perhaps with the words of the preacher of the Old Testament ringing in his ears: "The day of death is better than the day of one's birth. It is better to go to the house of mourning, than to go to the house of feasting: for that is the end of all men" (Eccl. 7:1,2). So what is the point? "Let us also go, that we may die with Him."

We meet Thomas again in the upper room. Jesus talks to His disciples. They listen in silence: "You must not let yourselves be distressed—you must hold on to your faith in God and your faith in me. There are many rooms in my

Father's house. If there were not, should I have told you that I am going away to prepare a place for you? It is true that I am going away to prepare a place for you, but it is just as true that I am coming again to welcome you into my own home, so that you may be where I am. You know where I am going and you know the road I am going to take" (Jn. 14:1-4, *Phillips*).

But the sullen and brooding Thomas airs his question: "Lord, we do not know where you're going, and how can we know what road you're going to take?" (Jn. 14:5, *Phillips*). He cannot be put off with words. He must know for himself. He asks a factual question. "*Where* are you going? *How* can we know the way?"

And Jesus replies: "I myself am the road, and the truth and the life (Jn. 14:6, *Phillips*). No one approaches the Father except through me." Where am I going?—to the Father. What is the way?—I am. How can you find it?—through Me. Thomas received more than he asked for. Christ is the way to God, the truth in His person, the life as it ought to be lived.

We meet Thomas once more on Easter Sunday. Jesus has risen from the dead. He has appeared to Mary. He makes His appearance to the apostles, to all the apostles except two—Judas, who is dead, and Thomas, who is absent. Why was Thomas missing? He was likely so moody and melancholy, so pessimistic and upset that he could not bear to see his friends. He retreated into a shell. He lived continually with his frustration, his disappointment, his disillusionment. He was absent when Jesus appeared!

Think of all he missed! He missed the vision of the risen Christ. He missed the words Jesus spoke. He missed the hope of Easter. He missed seeing the Truth and the Life. He missed the fellowship of other believers.

On this all-too-short journey of life we miss so much. We miss faith and hope and growth in maturity every time we fail to worship. We miss the presence of God, the pardon of Christ, the courage to resist temptation, the hope that smiles in the face of suffering, the vision that lifts us out of despair, the victory that is triumphant over death. No wonder our faith remains as outmoded and rusty as a worn out '66 Rambler, ready for the junk heap, instead of being alive and vital.

Inasmuch as he was absent, he would not believe the news. The others told him that they had seen the risen Jesus, that He was alive. He would never believe that! He knew they were trustworthy men, but now he would not trust them. He knew they were honorable, but he would not honor their word. He felt guilty, his conscience bothered him, and in his guilt he became defiant:

"Unless I see the mark of the nails on his hands, unless I put my finger into the place where the nails were, and my hand into his side, I will not believe it" (Jn. 20:25, *NEB*).

This is less than a man of little faith. This is a man of virtually no faith! This is not a doubting Thomas. This is a dejected, skeptical, stubborn Thomas. He is arrogant and insulting toward Christ! But he does say: "Except . . . " He leaves room for one condition, one exception. God must answer that prayer. God must meet that condition.

A week goes by. Every day the others talk to Thomas. Again and again he refuses to join them, to pray with them. What a battle for the mulish Thomas. But after much persuasion, the next Sunday he goes with them to their meeting place.

And Jesus appears! He surrenders to the skeptic's stubbornness. He humbles Himself before the pessimistic doubter. He appears with the words Thomas himself had spoken—He knows those words— and repeats them now: "Thomas, 'reach your finger here: see my hands; reach your hand here and put it into my side; be unbelieving no longer, but believe'" (Jn. 20:27, *NEB*).

That is too much for Thomas. In one stroke he is turned from foe to friend, from denier to confessor, from doubter to believer. More, he surpasses all the other apostles with his confession on his knees: *"My Lord and my God!"* (Jn. 20:28). It is reserved for this sullen skeptic to come to the most *shining* faith! He does not experiment. He does not put his finger into the wounds. It is not necessary!

Despite all his doubts and fears, Thomas arrived on solid ground. Now nothing is so firmly established for him, as that which he once doubted. Tradition says that he preached in India where he became a martyr. Yes— "There lives more faith in honest doubt, believe me, than in half the creeds."

Jesus said something else to Thomas—and He said it for us. It was His last word to the doubter-turned-believer: "Because you have seen me you have found faith. Happy are they who never saw me and yet have found faith" (Jn. 20:29, *NEB*). If that means anything, it means that there is no advantage for the apostles and no disadvantage for us! No excuse to say: "This is not fair. They saw Him; we do not see Him. If we cannot see Him, how does He expect us to believe?"

What is faith? Faith is not sight. Faith is the opposite of sight. Thomas not only had faith, he had sight: "Because you have seen me you have found faith." Faith is: "Happy are they who never saw me and yet have found faith." They who believe, shall *see*.

Visiting the Holy Land was a great experience for me. I saw places Jesus saw. I walked where He walked. But I did not see Jesus heal. I did not hear Jesus preach. I had no vision of the risen Christ. I saw only the brown mountains, the pale desert, the blue waters of the Sea of Galilee, but *Him* I did not see. There is no advantage in being there or here. Nor is there an advantage between being an apostle or living today. "Happy are they who never saw me and yet have found faith." If you want to deal with your doubts, if you will wrestle with your guilty conscience, if you have the curiosity to find out for yourself, you can find freedom at the feet of the risen Christ. Even a doubting Thomas can find it there—"My Lord and my God"—by *faith*. "Faith gives substance to our hopes, and makes us certain of realities we do not see. Without faith it is impossible to please him; for anyone who comes to God must believe that he exists and that he rewards those who search for him." (See Heb. 11:1,6.)

Faith is no mere intellectual assent. Faith is a "radical conviction influencing decisively and forever the trend and direction of a man's life . . . The very faith which is the upward reach of man's soul comes from without, and is a gift of God . . . The human heart does not produce it. God bestows it . . . The human spirit encounters the living God revealed in Christ, recognizing with endless wonder the holy love that has been yearning for it from the foundation of the world and has come forth to meet it, and yields itself to that seeking and implacable love, not grudgingly nor with many a reservation and doubt, but deliberately and vehemently and forever."*

Christ is risen. He appeared to the apostles. He

---

* James S. Stewart, *A Man in Christ pp. 180-3, Harper & Row.*

appeared to Thomas. There is no question about it. There is evidence enough. The whole Christian religion is built on the Lordship of the risen Christ. So yours is a choice, the choice of faith: "Life's business being just the terrible choice."* Terrible, if wrong. Not terrible, but full of joy if rightly made.

The risen Son of God—the living Lord—stands before us, hands outstretched, wounds visible, and says: "Reach your finger here: see my hands; reach your hand here and put it into my side; be unbelieving no longer, but believe. Happy are they who never saw me and yet have found faith."

* * * * * * * * * * * * *

The Acts of Thomas, written during the second century, record the division of the world. Each apostle was given a portion for his ministry, and Thomas was accorded India. Stubborn, as always, Thomas at first refused to go. Then in a vision he dreamed he was sold as a slave to an Indian merchant. Realizing God's will for his life, he went in obedience to his Lord's command.

Whether Thomas ever labored in India is questionable. Some traditions fix his missionary endeavors in Parthia and Persia, while other sources take him farther East. The Malabar Christians of St. Thomas in India still count him as their first evangelist and martyr. Some traditions say that he was shot by a shower of arrows while praying. Whatever his manner of death, the Doubter had found life worth giving.

* Robert Browning, *The Ring and the Book, Sec. 10, "The Pope," Line 1231 from Sermons Preached in a University Church*, p. 150 Abingdon Press, N.Y. & Nashville, 1959.

13

The Apostle Paul

The Great One

I am deeply grateful to Jesus Christ (to whom I owe all that I have accomplished) for trusting me enough to appoint me His minister, despite the fact that I had previously blasphemed His name, persecuted His Church, and damaged His cause . . . Jesus Christ entered the world to rescue sinners. I realize that I was the worst of them all . . . (I Tim. 1:12-15, Phillips).

It was the most far-fetched religious nonsense he had ever heard! How anyone in his right mind could even believe it, he would never understand. Ridiculous, incredible tales!

He was no dumbbell. He had heard religious fancies before. He was a student of religion, and he had studied with the best. Had he not sat at the feet of the finest teachers of the law? Had he not studied long and hard the best theologians? He had sorted the credible from the incredible, the possible from the impossible, the believable from the unbelievable.

Besides, he had examined all the Greek legends. No one could ever accuse him of not knowing. But these were myths about gods; not about men. No one in his right mind ever believed that Apollos or Hercules were anything but legendary. On the other hand, Aristotle and Socrates were great men —and nothing more.

This fanciful imagination about Jesus of Nazareth . . . what did they try to say about Him? That He was a man no one denied. He had been born in Bethlehem and grew up in Nazareth. Everybody knew that. He attracted a following—at first. He healed people, worked miracles, helped those who came to him. Paul had heard all about that, nor did he dispute it. His own colleagues attested it. Jesus had done many miracles.

Yes, but the man was not a trained theologian; just an itinerant self-styled preacher. He had no college education, no seminary experience and had only been baptized by that wild preacher, John—may God rest his prophetic soul. From what he had heard about the man's teaching, he had to agree that Jesus had something to say. It was, of course, all based on the law. Jesus was acquainted with Moses and the prophets, and yet there was an originality about Him—an authority—but that was all.

When at last He got Himself into trouble, tried to clean out the temple grounds, that was too much! What right had He in there? What authority did He have? Naturally Caiaphas had done the right thing by handing Him over to die. Crucifixion was a terrible way to go. But, then, who did Jesus think He was anyway?

And now this claptrap about Jesus' resurrection! His

disciples preaching that Jesus came back from the dead! They must be out of their minds! Resurrection? A Greek mythological notion, a belief borrowed from the mystery religions of Isis or Mithra, and, at best, a possible event at the end of time. Recently it had become a doctrine among the Pharisees—but at the end of the world!

There were gods many, and lords many, but only ONE GOD of the Hebrews. And Jesus? A Jewish carpenter, that was all. A good man, a teacher, maybe a prophet, but also a troublemaker. Not really a devout Jew! He broke the sabbath day deliberately, did not attend the synagogue regularly during His last year, offered forgiveness to all sorts of riff-raff and disrupted the temple. No, not a serious Jew.

Jesus—resurrected? These ignorant fishermen from Galilee must be silenced. They don't know what they're talking about. Superstition—that's all it is. Superstitious dreaming. How can they affirm Jesus as the Messiah? Why it's blasphemy!

As a learned son, as a man who has studied the law, as a devout Hebrew and religious leader of the strict sect of the Pharisees, he, Paul, had vowed to exterminate this heresy. He could not tolerate it. And the God of Israel, the true and living God, would be pleased with his zealous labors. What better way to devote one's life than to fight heresy and extinguish heretics! He would go wherever he could to find these believers in Jesus. He would bring them before the authorities and expose their fiction. They could not stand up in court. They could never defend their views before the orthodox. Their fanciful dreams would be exposed before the truth—and the scriptures of law and prophecy would triumph.

One of those poor deluded believers had even been

stoned, and he, Paul, had been there. He had seen it all. This man had tried to preach—had tried to tell them, the Pharisees, of Jewish history. He had even dared to accuse them: "How stubborn you are, heathen still at heart and deaf to the truth! You always fight against the Holy Spirit. Like fathers, like sons. Was there ever a prophet whom your fathers did not persecute? They killed those who foretold the coming of the Righteous One; and now you have betrayed him and murdered him" (Acts 7:51-53, *NEB*).

That was too much. They turned on him then. And he himself had heard that terrible blasphemy, as Stephen said: "I can see the Son of Man standing at God's right hand" (Acts 7:56, *NEB*). They had stoned him right there and then, and Paul witnessed the deed.

Now he was on his way to Damascus. He had official papers from Jerusalem. He could search out these heretics and propagators of foolishness and bring them down forcibly to Jerusalem. Jesus, the Son of Man? Risen from the dead? At God's right hand? Preposterous. *How* could a man rise from the dead? *How* could He come back from the grave? And with what body? A dead body alive? Ascend into heaven? How? Go up in space—to God—to His right hand? Blasphemy, sheer blasphemy! "Hear, O Israel, the Lord our God is *one* Lord" (Deut. 6:4). *ONE!* How could any man ascend to *GOD?* God is one. There is none else. If these people really believe this babble they must be very simple, stupid—no, deranged!

In spite of the fact that he knew his cause was right, he kept on thinking, as he traveled with his friends, whether he was going about this in the right way. If there was one thing he knew of Jesus' teaching it was his emphasis on love. But should one love a heresy? Could anyone accept falsehood? Surely the prophets themselves denounced false prophets.

Yet, what if Jesus were the Messiah? What if he were the Deliverer? And rejected, as the simpleton—what was his name?—Stephen had said. What if Jesus had risen and . . . ? There was that prophecy: "Thou wilt not leave my soul in hell; neither wilt thou suffer thine Holy One to see corruption" (Ps. 16:10). No, that could not be applied to Jesus! The whole thing was obviously a fraud!

Suddenly, there, above him, as brilliant as the noonday sun, he saw a light. It was brighter than the sun. What was this? A vision? He fell to the ground. The light was overpowering— blinding—he could not see.

"Saul, Saul, why are you persecuting Me?"

A Voice! Calling him by name.

"Who are you, Lord?"

He could barely get the words out.

"I am Jesus whom you are persecuting. But now stand up and go into the city and there you will be told what you must do" (Acts 9:4-6, *Phillips*).

The vision was over. As suddenly as it had come, it was gone.

"Did you hear that?" Paul said to his traveling companions, as he arose.

"Hear what?"

"The Voice. Did you hear the Voice?

"No, but we saw a Light."

"And you heard nothing?"

"Nothing. Did you hear anything?"

"Yes . . . the Voice said: 'Saul, Saul, why are you persecuting Me?'"

"You—persecuting *God*?"

"No—it was Jesus."

"*Jesus?* What are you talking about?"

"I heard a Voice which said: 'I am Jesus Whom you are persecuting. Go into the city and there you will be told what you must do.'"

"We heard nothing!"

"Where are you? I can't see you."

"What do you mean you can't see us, Saul?"

"Can *you* see all right?"

"Yes. Of course."

"I'm blinded. Help me. We must go on to Damascus."

In Damascus he took a room and kept to himself. He prayed and fasted. He had no sight for three days. Over and over he pondered the vision. He had seen Jesus—no questions about that—He must be alive! He must be the Messiah, the risen Lord. He has ascended. He has power at the right hand of God. Incredible and mysterious as it all sounded to him—it was all true, as Stephen had said. No fool, this Stephen. He had seen the Son of Man, too. (See I Cor. 15:8.) It was gloriously *true!*

After three days a Jew in good standing in the community, but also a believer in Jesus, knocked on his door. He announced: "Saul, brother, you may see again!" As miraculously as he had lost his sight, it returned. He blinked his eyes a couple of times to make sure.

"The God of our fathers has chosen you to know his will, to see the righteous one, to hear words from his own lips, so that you may become his witness before all men of what you have seen and heard. And now what are you waiting for? Get up and be baptized! Be clean from your sins as you call on his name (Acts 22:13-16, *Phillips*).

Baptized? Baptized by the followers of Jesus? !

Paul felt constrained to enter the synagogue on the next Sabbath. Here, he faced the Jewish community. He, the Pharisee from Jerusalem who had been sent for the express purpose of exterminating this heresy about Jesus, told what had happened to him on the road to Damascus. He told his story, announced his conversion and proclaimed Jesus as the Messiah, the risen Lord. Why, the Scripture had said: "Neither wilt thou suffer thine Holy One to see corruption." He had doubted that himself, but it *was* so!

They were astonished, dumbfounded. He met with them again. He went into every synagogue. It was all too much for them. They were so greatly upset that some plotted to take his life. When the believers found out about it they helped Paul escape.

It had happened with such dramatic suddenness, that he went into the desert to meditate. What had happened to him? What would this vision do to his life—his purpose for living? Everything was changed. Everything was new. It was time to rethink his life, his future. He took out his familiar Bible and started to pore over it again. This time it was with new eyes, this time with a understanding, as if led by the Spirit of God. He was beginning really to see for the first time,

He read again the life of his favorite character, Abraham. What was it about Abraham that made him a great man? Was it his knowledge of the law on which he, Paul, had always prided himself? No! Abraham lived before God gave the law and commandments. How was Abraham considered righteous then, if not by the law? Suddenly he saw it. The sentence hit him as never before. It had been there all the time, but now it made sense: Abraham believed God and it was counted unto him for righteousness. If Abraham had been justified by works, he had something of which to be proud. But surely not before God. He believed

God's promise and was strong in faith: "And being fully persuaded that, what he had promised, he was able also to perform . . . it was imputed to him for righteousness" (Rom. 4:2,3,20-22—based on Gen. 15:6).

Now he reconsidered the law of Moses. He had always tried to live by God's commandments. He felt he had kept the law and was blameless. Everyone considered him a good Jew—a good religious man—ethical, pure, righteous. And he was even a fighter for God, zealous of good works. But what had all this done to him? He was not as good as everyone thought him to be. He knew his own shortcomings. Secretly he hoped that his persecution of the believers in Jesus might result in recognition from the authorities. They might admire him, promote him. And what had it all done to his spirit? He had become hard— relentless—so assured of doing God's will. He could stand there and watch them stone that man in cold self-righteousness!

The law had not made him righteous. It had not made him acceptable to God no matter how much he fooled himself. He was ignorant of God's righteousness, going about to establish his own. What had Moses really said about the law? "Curse is on all who do not persevere in doing everything that is written in the Book of the Law" (Gal. 3:10— based on Deut. 27:26, *NEB*). Everything? No, he had not done everything. There must be a better way as Abraham found. By faith? Habakkuk!—"He shall gain life who is justified through faith" (Gal 3:11—based on Hab. 2:4, *NEB*)! So then, "it is evident that no one is ever justified before God in terms of law . . . law is not at all a matter of having faith: . . . Christ bought us freedom from the curse of the law by becoming for our sake an accursed thing; for Scripture says, 'Cursed is everyone who is hanged on a tree.' If a law had been given which had Power to bestow life, then indeed righteousness would have come from keeping the law . . . the law was a kind of tutor in charge of us until Christ should come, when we should be justified through faith; and now that faith has come, the tutor's charge is at an end" (Gal. 3:12,13,21,24,25, *NEB*). Christ is the end of the law for righteousness!

So now, forgetting the things which were behind, he had to forge ahead to new goals. He had been arrested by Jesus on the road to Damascus. He could never go back. He left Arabia in the Spirit and went to Jerusalem to meet the apostles. He gathered all available information about the life of Jesus, His death and resurrection.

Then he was soon thrust into the thick of it: Antioch, Cyprus, Lystra, Derbe, Ephesus, Troas, Philippi, Thessalonica, Athens, Corinth, back to Jerusalem—Rome. Jew, Greek, Roman, barbarian, slave and free, all felt the impact of this man of God.

The story of the early Church is an exciting story. It is a story of Paul and the other apostles, who turned the world upside down. Nothing would ever be the same again! If we look back on this first-century revolution, it is obvious that ever advance of civilization and cultural achievement is due to Jesus Christ and to the fervency with which these men proclaimed Him. They told the good news. They were empowered by God's Spirit. They burned with a holy passion.

In less than one generation a obscure event in Palestine became the number one topic of conversation throughout the Roman Empire.

This was not the usual revolution—not a revolution with weapons of war but in "weakness" of preaching. Not with pride and pomp but with purity of heart and motive.

Not with arms but with ardor. Neither was it merely an intellectual revolution. These were not simply new ideas or a different ideology; not just a philosophy or even a way of life. It was pure and simple news: good news—and *what* news!

God came in Jesus. He visited our planet. Jesus is promised Messiah and Lord of life. How can the world ever be the same now? This is *the* event among all events. He willingly died on our behalf. He died for our sins. He rose again from the dead. "Since by man came death, by man came also the resurrection of the dead" (I Cor. 15:21).

Paul was a changed man. And no one he met could ever forget him or his new-found faith. It was this *faith* which changed Paul. The living reality of Christ was his message. That was all. "We preach Christ crucified" (I Cor. 1:23).

Wherever he went he stirred up violent reactions. He was persecuted, assaulted, threatened, beaten, imprisoned, attacked, pursued, stoned, blasphemed, ridiculed, bound with chains and shipwrecked.

What thrilling stories these. Never was a town the same after Paul's visit. They would not all be Christians. Far from it. But the issues were clear-cut. Christ believed on or Christ rejected. Christ the Way or Christ the stumblingblock! They all knew Paul had been there and few remained indifferent. If they were not passionately for him, they were violently against him. There were no ifs, ands, and buts. Only either—or. Thus the stonings and beatings and constant attacks. He did turn the world upside down. His message brought the conflict between the Word of God and the life of man out into the open.

But . . . did he really turn the world upside down? Wouldn't you rather say that he turned the world rightside up? Had not the world—this fallen world—turned away from God? Was it not upside down already? Wouldn't you say that he turned the world rightside up?

And that is your conflict, too. Is your life upside down or rightside up? What are your values, your ideas, your goals? And if anyone should come to you with this message to change your life, to repent, to leave off establishing your goodness and receive God's gift of life, wouldn't you react violently too? If your world is upside down, Christ must turn it up and over. That is a revolution. As it happened in the first century, so it must happen in the twentieth!

Little wonder that his last months were lived out in prison after prison until he died a martyr's death in Rome. Through all of this he remained optimistic, bright, faithful, joyous. He was delivered from despair and called himself more than a conqueror. How? He knew the darkness, but also saw the light. He felt his human weaknesses, but also experienced the grace of God. He lived with death, but all the while Life coursed through him:

"Wherever we go we carry death with us in our body, the death that Jesus died, that in this body also life may reveal itself, the life that Jesus lives . . . I have been crucified with Christ; the life I now live is not my life, but the life which Christ lives in me; and my present bodily life is lived by faith in the Son of God, who loved me and sacrificed himself for me . . . For to me life is Christ, and death gain" (II Cor. 4:10; Gal. 2:20; Phil. 1:21, *NEB*).

Paul the apostle, was God's chosen instrument in Judas' Place. Justifiably, Paul considered himself a apostle, too:

> *Last of all he was seen of me also, as of one born out of due time. For I am the least of the apostles, that am not meet to be called an apostle, because I persecuted the church of God. But by the grace of God I am what I am: and his grace which was bestowed upon me was not in vain; but I labored more abundantly than they all: yet not I, but the grace of God which was with me . . . so we preach, and so ye believed* (I Cor. 15:8-11).

*   *   *   *   *   *   *   *   *   *   *   *   *

According to tradition, the apostle Paul was beheaded three miles outside of the old Rome. On that site is the beautiful basilica St. Paul's Outside the Walls, with a statue of the apostle in front.

As for me, I feel that the last drops of my life are being poured out for God. The glorious fight that God gave me I have fought, the course that I was set I have finished, and I have kept the faith, The future for me holds the crown of righteousness which God, the true judge, will give to me in that day—and not, of course, only to me but to all those who have loved what they have seen of him.

In my opinion whatever we may have to go through now is less than nothing compared with the magnificent future God has planned for us. The whole creation is on tiptoe to see the wonderful sight of the sons of God coming into their own.

If God is for us, who can be against us? He that did not grudge his own Son but gave him up for us all—can we not trust such a God to give us, with him, everything else that we can need?

Can anything separate us from the love of Christ? I have become absolutely convinced that neither death nor life, neither messenger of Heaven nor monarch of earth, neither what happens today nor what may happen tomorrow, neither a power from on high nor a power from below, nor anything else in God's whole world has any power to separate us from the love of God in Jesus Christ our Lord (II Tim 4:6-8; Rom. 8:18,19,31,32,35, 38,39, *Phillips)!*

Apostle and Disciple

A disciple is one who learns;
An apostle is one who is sent.

A disciple receives a message;
An apostle transmits a message.

There were many disciples;
There were but few apostles.

There are many learners;
There are few witnesses.

We must know before we can tell;
We need to tell what we know.

Learning is the basis for living.
A changed life is the fruit of learning.

Jesus needs disciples before He can
have "apostles."

Jesus wants to make "apostles" out of
His disciples!

"Just as the Father sent Me,
So I am going to send you."*

*Jn. 20:21, *Phillips.*